From Pyecombe to Cuckfield

With Stops Along the Way

MARK DUDENEY AND EILEEN HALLETT

Illustrated by Mark Dudeney

Mid-Sussex Books

CW01655609

First published in 1999 by

Mid-Sussex Books
4 Crescent Road
Burgess Hill
West Sussex
RH15 8EG

© 1999 Mid Sussex Books
Illustrations © 1999 Mark Dudeney

ISBN 0 9530625 8 6

All rights reserved. No part of this publication may be reproduced, stored in a retrieval system, or transmitted, in any form or by any means, electronic, mechanical, photocopying, recording or otherwise, without the prior permission of the Publisher.

Printed in Great Britain by
Delta Press
2 Goldstone Street
Hove Sussex BN3 3RJ

The photograph on the front cover depicts the late Bob Upton who was the shepherd at Wayfield Farm, Pyecombe for many years. His father, grandfather and great-grandfather were all shepherds before him.

Acknowledgements

The authors gratefully acknowledge the sources from which they have drawn their information, all are appropriately referred to in the text. In particular they wish to thank the following organisations and individuals for their generous help and assistance:

Cassells plc, for allowing us to quote an extract from a description of Clayton Windmills that appears in *My Life and Soft Times* by Henry Longhurst

Robert Hale Ltd, for allowing us to quote an extract from an interview with Charles Mitchell, as well as an observation on windmills, both of which appear in *Small Talk in Sussex* by Esther Meynell

Extracts and a photograph of the author's father are reproduced by kind permission from *Magnus Volk of Brighton* by Conrad Volk, published in 1971 by Phillimore and Co. Ltd., Chichester, West Sussex

The Editor and staff of the *Hassocks and Keymer Talk About* for allowing us to quote so extensively from the magazine

Mr Derrick Ayton, for allowing us to quote from his History of the Weald Lawn Tennis and Squash Rackets Club

Mr John Hayward for allowing us to quote from his unpublished history of *Sussex Roads and Turnpikes*

Miss Valerie Raynor-Smith, for permission to use a photograph of the Weald Lawn Tennis Club that was taken by her grandfather and founder member, the late Mr W. O. Pratt

Brighton Public Library for permission to use a photograph of Magnus Volk's sea-going car on the Rottingdean Railway

Burgess Hill Public Library

Mrs Marilyn Arbon – Curator of the Cuckfield Museum

Mr Frederick Avery – Curator of the Burgess Hill Local History Society

Mr Rupert Ayton; Mrs Eileen Bennett; Mrs Jane Cragg; Mr Philip Dudeney; Mr Richard Dudeney; Dorothy and Barry Edwards; Mr T. Hedgecock; Mrs B. Higgins; Miss Lambard; Mr Geoffrey Lee; Mrs V. Long; Mr Jim Martin; Mr W. J. Mottram; Mrs J. Mugridge; Mrs Susan Muir; Mrs Mary Offer; Mr Ray Packham; Miss Rose Powell

Finally gratitude is extended to Rose Dudeney for her professional advice and editorial expertise and to Mark Leo Dudeney for the many hours spent converting our rough notes into presentable typescript.

Contents

Introduction

Change is in the air! The millennium approaches. And as a result of recent government decisions, it seems likely that the citizens of Mid Sussex will be celebrating the event while even more of their precious countryside is being buried under concrete!

The purpose of this publication therefore is to capture if it can, the essence of the area as it used to be, and to place on record some of the people, places and events that in different ways and at different times have helped to create the charm and character of the district that we know today.

In keeping with this theme, both the style and presentation of the book have been influenced by methods adopted by earlier writers who would often use the road to thread their narrative. In our case, it is the much travelled road that links the ancient hamlet of Pyecombe with the historical town of Cuckfield, and the stories that follow all share an affinity with that particular highway. As for the people who live along its route, they are mostly of Sussex extraction and so are naturally blessed with many sterling qualities! They also possess what ignorant folk ascribe as being an infuriating streak of stubbornness, but which in reality is a sensible and deep rooted determination not to be chivvied into making hasty decisions. A characteristic that is neatly summed up by the following well known lines:

Some folks as comes to Sussex,
They reckon as they knows,
A durn sight better what to do
Than simple folks like me and you
could possibly suppose.
But them as comes to Sussex
They mustn't push and shove
For Sussex will be Sussex
And Sussex wunt be druv.

To such people then, the true natives of the county, those that 'wunt be druv', we respectfully dedicate this work.

Pyecombe

The Ancient Road ~ The Church ~ Blacksmiths ~ Shepherds ~ The Golf Course

Situated high on the South Downs, the parish of Pyecombe thrusts out peninsular-like above and between two busy roads. On its western flank lies the A23, the main thoroughfare connecting London with Brighton, and a route upon which a near constant stream of traffic produces a deafening din for all of the day and most of the night. Then forking off from this noisy highway and thus forming the eastern boundary of the community, is the other road (our road) which after skirting the local golf course, heads over the hill to Clayton.

But this is the modern scene. Time was when travellers heading either north or south had no choice but to pass through the hamlet along the narrow street that to this day links the Plough Inn with the Church. It is a truly ancient road, one that was in use long before the Norman invasion, one that was old in Roman times, and one that in all probability is older than Pyecombe itself. It leads on from the Church, passes a few cottages and then reverts to a chalk track that rises gently up to the brow of the hill where a jumble of paths criss-cross it in various directions. These too are old, and some much older than others.

The Plough Inn – a well known staging post which in its time served as the local court as well as a temporary mortuary

The track widens to a more substantial green way at this point, and then veers round the side of a coombe in the direction of the Clayton Windmills. This section is believed to be a remnant of the famous Tin Road, so called because in the days of antiquity, when the Phoenicians brought trade to these shores, it was the route by which the tin ore they sought, was transported overland from the Cornish mines to Pevensey and the east.

In more recent times – 1775 or thereabouts – because of the growing popularity of Brighton (or Brighthelmstone as it was then called) it was felt that the town should be linked more directly with the capital. Therefore the existing track was upgraded by act of parliament to a turnpike, and whereas before, coaches had either followed the coast to Shoreham or crossed the hills to Lewes before venturing inland, they instead went directly north via Patcham to Pyecombe.

From there they went up past the Inn and the Church, then a short distance along the old Tin Road before descending the hill to Clayton. This section (which was probably Roman in origin) ran roughly parallel with the present day highway, and being particularly precipitous in places, must have presented a daunting challenge to horse-drawn vehicles, and it is not difficult to imagine the trepidation of the passengers as they were hauled over such rough terrain. Nor would they have extracted much comfort from studying the recommended safety procedures that are nicely described in *Chambers Information for the People* :

> Should the horses run off, sit perfectly still, and in anticipation of the possible overturn, keep your legs and arms from straggling. Sit easily and compactly, so that when upset, you will gently roll over in the direction you are thrown. We have seen ladies in these circumstances scream wildly and throw their arms out of the windows, thus exposing themselves to the chance of broken

Pyecombe

limbs. Never jump from a rapidly moving vehicle unless, supposing it impossible to slip down behind, you see a precipice in front, in which case any risk of personal damage is preferable to remaining still. The Duke of Orleans lost his life by neglecting these simple precautions!

Details of the Duke's demise were not described, but the message was clear, and one can imagine the relief felt by the southbound passenger, when having surmounted the hill, the Plough Inn, the last but one staging post on their journey, came into view.

Exposed to all the winds that blow, Pyecombe could never be described as a pretty village. Its beauty lies more in the sweeping downs that surround it, for in itself it is a hotch-potch sort of place, being in a sense, two hamlets, not one. Indeed a visitor viewing the southern half could be excused for thinking that he was looking at the neighbourhood in its entirety. But he would be deceived, for half a mile along the Albourne Road – up it pops again!

The reason for this divergence is supposed to have stemmed from a time when the inhabitants found themselves suddenly faced with the threat of the plague, and it is thought that the consequent fear of contagion caused many of them to beat a hasty retreat to the north. Whether in so doing they managed to avoid the epidemic is uncertain, but that an evacuation occurred is at least partly supported by the study of old photographs of the area. They clearly show the Inn and the Church, but little else, and as it seems unlikely that such gathering places would have stood in isolation, the suggestion of a previous shift of population could well be right.

It must also be said, that apart from the small Norman Church with its massive buttresses, the district contains few buildings of architectural interest, unless of course one counts the line of ventilation shafts that betray the presence of the railway tunnel buried deep below. The Church should be viewed as in it there is much that is worth seeing, particularly a fine lead font, which it is said, dates back to the twelfth century, thereby making it as old as the building itself.

There is a good story about this particular artifact and one that is well worth recording. It would appear that during the time of the English Civil War, in 1645 or thereabouts, the 'Cromwellites' were melting down all of the lead they could find in order to make bullets for the military. Dwellings were entered and searched without so much as a 'by your leave', and any lead utensils found within were confiscated for the cause. Churches were also searched and much that was sacred was destroyed. But fortunately for posterity, the Warden at Pyecombe was too sharp for the pilfering Roundheads, and before they arrived, he daubed the receptacle with whitewash, thus giving it the appearance of stone. To his eternal credit, the subterfuge worked and the font was saved for future generations to immerse their offspring. It is claimed that traces of the selfsame whitewash remain on it to this very day.

Despite such goings-on, Pyecombe's real claim to fame lies not so much in its Church, or geographical location, but in the shepherd's crooks (or sheep hooks) that were once made there. It is these implements more than anything else, that are associated with both the district and the blacksmiths who over the years have worked at the village forge. To a shepherd, this item was all-important, indeed his living depended on its skilful use, it was – apart from his dog – the most essential thing he possessed. With it he could catch a sheep by the hind leg, or a lamb by the neck – without it he could catch nothing!

Although many smiths were noted for crook-making in the area in which they worked, a certain number gained a wider reputation, and amongst these was one named Berry, who during the nineteenth century became famous for the quality of his Pyecombe hooks. This tradition of excellence was to be continued and improved upon by Charles Mitchell (the 'smith of smiths') who worked at the same forge for over sixty years. His crooks, which were similar to Berry's but more refined, are considered by those who know, to be the finest examples of the craft yet seen, and as such are keenly sought by collectors the world over, and amongst their numbers are many church bishops, who regard the possession of a Mitchell crook to be an indispensable feature of their regalia.

Pyecombe Church – the original name of which has been lost in the mists of time

Looking east from Church Lane. The chimney-like structure is one of the railway tunnel ventilation shafts. Workmen in wicker baskets were lowered down through these whilst construction was in progress

Numbers 6, 7, 8 and 9 Church Cottages before they were demolished in the 1930s. Pyecombe forge is to the left of the picture

In the following extract from her book *Small Talk in Sussex*, Esther Meynell describes an occasion when she visited the Pyecombe forge and spoke to Mr Mitchell:

> The forge at Pyecombe is a large one; it had to be, as it did a lot of trade in its heyday. It has many cross-beams hung with horse shoes. A capacious brick chimney goes up in the middle, the wooden handle of the bellows stretching out at the side. There were two anvils and a curious rough old stool, hollow in the middle, rather like two blunt horseshoes joined together – I forgot to ask what it was for – and a great heap of battered old iron collected at one side.
>
> Laid across the beams was an arrangement of two wooden poles whose use I enquired. I was told it was used in the old days for the shoeing of oxen. The ox, not being so sensible as the horse in lifting up his hoof, had to be thrown when he was shod and his legs tied to these poles. Many oxen have been shod in the past in this Pyecombe forge.
>
> "People asks I if I ever shod any oxen," old Mitchell remarked as I was looking at the poles. And I tells 'em 'underds. They doänt belieft I!,'"he added, smiling. "But I has, 'underds!"
>
> Mr Mitchell, when I visited him, was not far from his hundredth year and was still making the famous Pyecombe crooks so long linked with his name. He was a small old man, but he could still wield a three-pound hammer quicker than his son, as his son told me with pride. Long ago he came to Pyecombe from London, where he was born, though his father was a Sussex man, by stagecoach – the old coaching road ran past the forge down an incredibly steep bit of hill – in the days when railways were rarities, and he had been at Pyecombe ever since.
>
> In his quiet way he is very proud of his crooks.
>
> "I've made over two 'undred o' they," he said to me, touching the gracefully moulded head of the crook with his cunning old fingers. "I reckon as how my price for a-making' they crooks be dree-ha'pence an hour – but I doän't tell folks that!"

Mr Mitchell also made sheep-bells. These were fashioned out of any old iron that came to hand, even ancient gun barrels, and to give them a distinctive tone, he would beat in a quantity of brass, causing it to lay in big flakes in the iron. A set of sheep bells numbered between eighteen and twenty-one, and they ranged in tone from the big tenor, which measured five or six inches across, to the quite small and highly pitched trebles. They were generally regarded as being the property of the shepherd.

Charles Mitchell
(from a sketch by Juliet Somers that appeared in The Sussex County Magazine)

Referring to these bells in his book, *Off the Beaten Track in Sussex*, Arthur Stanley Cooke says:

> To those who think they have merely the one purpose to prevent straying, it may be interesting to learn that musical considerations enter into the custom. Thus however haphazard the sounds may seem to the listener, the intention is to make music and form chords.

Which is a rather controversial assumption – but there is surely no disputing what follows:

> Listen to the broken melody of the sheep-bells wafted across the slopes and hollows – like the skyward song of the lark, or the drone of the humble bee, it enters so completely into the spirit of the scene, that often only those unused to the sound will hear it. To me it is one of the sweetest sounds in nature.

The following anecdote concerning these instruments was written by Barclay Wills, a great authority on all matters connected with the South Downs. It appeared in *The Sussex County Magazine* in 1933, and at the time he, Mr Wills, was paying a visit to Nelson Coppard, the shepherd at Pangdean Farm:

> There is always something of interest or something quaint to note down after a visit to Nelson. Today, as I stood on the hill by Pyecombe Church, I could see his fold at the edge of Pangdean Farm. I was not expecting to hear much music from the sheep-bells, knowing that it is his custom to remove most of them and keep them in his hut at this time of year. I was therefore startled by the deafening burst of sound which greeted me as I approached the fold. The din did not stop until I actually passed the first barrier of wattles and furze branches. Behind these I found the shepherd and his son-in-law, Ted Nutley, holding the bells and laughing heartily at their success in 'ringin me in'.
>
> "I was just taking the bells into the hut,'" explained Nelson, "when Nutley saw you coming along. I know you like to hear the bells when you come, so we rung 'em for ye!"

Nelson Coppard, the son of a shepherd who worked on Dyke Hill, was born at Poynings in 1863 and started work very early as a shepherd boy. He served under several masters before securing the post at Pangdean. As Barclay Wills wrote:

> To write a full account of Mr Coppard as I know him would be a long story. He was the first shepherd I ever met. From him I had my first instruction on sheep-bells, crooks and the details of a

Nelson Coppard

> shepherd's life. To the lucky natives of Sussex, a meeting with a shepherd is just an ordinary incident in a Downland ramble, but to a Londoner blessed with an artistic temperament, that first sudden entry into a little valley full of sheep with their ancient bells chiming, the meeting with a jovial shepherd with his glittering crook, the chat with him and the return journey, when I carried home wild flowers and two large canister bells, was overwhelming. I felt that I had stepped into a new world.

It is easy to understand the effect experienced by Mr Wills, for these bearded patriarchs, dressed in round smocks and wide felt hats, must have cut splendid, near Old Testament figures as they tended their flocks. And although simple men from humble backgrounds with little or no education at all, they were nevertheless, wise and compassionate in the ways of their world. Their loyalty was always to their charges, the sheep, and therefore to their masters, the farmers. While in return, these worthies treated their shepherds with the utmost respect – almost as equals in fact – relying nearly entirely upon their proffered advice and expertise.

A fine example of a shepherd's devotion to duty is contained in the following letter sent by S. E. Terry to *The Sussex County Magazine*:

> In view of the articles on Sussex shepherds by Mr Barclay Wills now appearing in the Sussex County Magazine, you may be interested in the following true incident.
>
> It was a Sunday afternoon when George Pearce, a Pyecombe shepherd with a flock of 750 ewes and lambs, slipped upon a bank near the old barn above the Pyecombe Golf Links and, as he thought, sprained his ankle. When he attempted to move, the pain was great, but there was no one in sight to render help. If he left the sheep they would do great damage to the crops and some of them would probably become 'blown' and die. He wanted to fulfil his duty, so he turned to his dog, Peggy, and said, "You must do the work now for I can't get about very well."
>
> The faithful dog rounded them up and moved them down the hill over the rough ground for a quarter of a mile and Pearce drove them the remaining quarter of a mile into the fold. Not until the lambs had been supplied with oats and cake to last until the next morning, and the hurdles had been securely pegged down, did the shepherd think of going home, which he reached with great pain and difficulty. On arrival at his cottage he collapsed, but refused to keep to his bed, as he said a sprain would cure itself. It was not until the following Saturday that he consulted a doctor, who sent him to the Sussex County Hospital for X-ray, when it was discovered that his leg was fractured. For weeks he lay between life and death, but his mind was full of peace, praise and thanksgiving to the 'Great Shepherd and Bishop of our souls'.
>
> At length he recovered and once more took up his crook and called his dog to follow him. "Why didn't you leave the sheep to look after themselves?" I asked him recently.
>
> "I couldn't do that," he replied. "I was in charge of the flock and it was only my duty to see them safely into the fold."

Over the years so many excellent shepherds have tended their sheep on the hills surrounding Pyecombe, that to list them all would be a prodigious task. There is one however who cannot be ignored, and he was Walter Wooler. Born at Alfriston in 1856, he came to Pyecombe at the age of three months, when his father secured the position of shepherd to a Mr Blaker, a post he held for many years. Walter's natural aptitude for the care of the sheep and the thorough training he received are demonstrated by the fact that at the age of sixteen years, he had sole charge of a flock of 500 ewes belonging to Mr Blaker.

Fifty eight years later he was shepherding still, and the following extracts have been taken from a long and fascinating account of his life, as written by Barclay Wills.

> At the top of the steep path which starts at the farm buildings opposite Pyecombe Post Office, I found Mr Walter Wooler, one of the oldest shepherds working in East Sussex.
>
> I was delighted to discover that I had arrived in time to see him mark his sheep and lambs ready for the Lewes sheep sale.
>
> A number of small hurdle pens next to the fold contained the different lots of animals, and leading from the largest one was a long pointed pen with a movable hurdle at the wide end for a door.

I entered the fold to watch the shepherd at his task. Near the long pen a little hollow held his fire. A brick on either side supported the iron bars on which stood a pot of hot pitch. Deftly the shepherd dipped the marking iron into the pitch, shook off the drips, leaned over the hurdles and marked the wool of one of the lambs packed in the narrow pen. A dozen times he did this, then, after resting the marking iron on the pot, he lifted the heavy pitching iron from its place at the point of the pen, thereby releasing a hurdle to allow the lambs to escape. Out they ran, all clearly marked with an M in a circle (the farmer's initials) and joined the others in the fold.

"Time ago I had a mate at these times," he said, " to hold the sheep and mend the fire and so on, but though it takes longer alone, I do it as well by packing them in the pen tightly so they can't run about." In course of conversation I asked if he had ever used a cave or a 'shepherd's bush' and found that he had used a hole in the bank 'like the beginning of a cave' for resting in at times. Some furze branches put round the outside improved it. He had also taken a billhook out with him sometimes to cut away a convenient bush so that he could back into it and put his big umbrella over him. A 'round frock' and white corduroys was his usual dress. With a smock and the aforementioned umbrella he was not afraid of a wet day.

I look back on my visit to Walter Wooler with delight. I remember his quiet courtesy and his kindly interest in my desire to record precious little details.The picture that remains with me is that of the black pitch pot on the little fire and the dear old shepherd by the long hurdle pen with the marking iron in his hand."

Walter Wooler died in 1936 in his eightieth year and in a touching tribute to his memory, a poem entitled 'Old Shepherd' by Ethel Talbot was published in *The Sussex County Magazine*.

Old Shepherd

And do you say old Wooler's dead,
And lies nigh Pyecombe? Eh,
He was a Shepherd you'll not see
The like of now. It seems to me
Things aren't the same today.

White-smocked and with that dog of his
He'd be off by day or night
Out from his tidy cottage...Look,
It stands nigh Pyecombe forge. His crook
Was fashioned there, all right!

I as a lad would follow him;
He taught me all I knew;
We'd search the Downs aye, many an hour
In Spring to find the orchis flower;
He loved all flowers that grew.

And many tales old Wooler'd tell-
The legends of the Down;
It was a treat to hear him talk,
Fossils he'd find too, in the chalk-
Even the Shepherd's Crown*.

But 'twere the sheep he loved the best;
Close to his heart they'd seem,
Them ewes have missed him I'll be bound
Since Wooler was laid underground
To rest, maybe and dream.

Well there is no one will deny
He's part of Sussex still;
He wasn't one who could forget
The Downs he loved: he loves them yet –
Wooler of Pyecombe Hill

*The Shepherd's Crown is a fossilised sea-urchin embedded in flint.

Walter Wooler

As stated earlier, our road lies on the eastern side of the community and runs past the golf course that was laid out on a stretch of downland between Pyecombe and Standean in 1894. It is certainly worth a visit, if only to enjoy the views from the links and with regard to these, by following the boundary path, one will eventually descend into a valley or a coombe. It will have been worth the exercise, for at that point a backward glance reveals a breathtaking panorama which not only encompasses the hamlet on the near horizon, but also includes an entrancing glimpse of the weald through the cleft between Wolstonbury and Newtimber Hills.

Closer to hand and on the other side of the boundary fence is a small pool artfully positioned so as to frustrate golfers on their approach to the green. Surrounded by clumps of rushes with water lilies floating on the surface, it is despite the presence of an artificial and rather unconvincing heron, very pretty, and lends a pleasing and civilised touch to the scene.

How times have changed – for many years ago, long before the existence of the golf course, this then remote and lonely spot was a favoured venue for cock fighting. An ancient and dried out dewpond was used as a sort of open air amphitheatre for those engaged in the practice, and within its saucer .shaped depression, unfortunate gamecocks fought each other to the death. Little imagination is required to picture the brutal goings-on, and it can be understood why precautions were taken to ensure the secrecy of the proceedings. In the event the locality was well chosen, as the surrounding hills not only muffled the excited uproar of the onlookers, but also provided vantage points for look-outs on guard against the arrival of the authorities.

Now it is all just history, and the dewpond apart, traces of which can still be seen, nothing remains to betray the dark secrets of those far-off days. But passions linger on – as every missed putt or sliced drive will readily reveal!

Clayton

The Windmills ~ Clayton Hill ~ The Lime Kilns ~ The Old Barn Meeting House ~ The Village and Church ~ The Seven Men ~ The Railway Tunnel and Disaster ~ The Matsfield Arms ~ The Suffragists ~ The Canadians

Having just passed the brow of the hill, a narrow road branches off sharply to the right. This leads to the Clayton windmills. With regard to such premises, Esther Meynell in her book *Small Talk in Sussex* ventures the opinion that:

> The idea of modern houses being built on the Downs fills the mind with horror. But there is one human structure that adds and does not subtract from the beauty, and that is a windmill.

How right she was, and the tower mill *Jack* with its neighbour, the post mill *Jill* were surely in her thoughts when she made the observation. The pair of them situated high on the Downs above the little hamlet of Clayton are undoubtedly amongst the best known rural sights in England, and Mrs Meynell, who lived in nearby Ditchling, could probably have seen them both from her bedroom window.

Another writer, R. Thurston Hopkins, in his book *Old Watermills and Windmills* states:

> The two most popular windmills in Sussex are Jack and Jill on Clayton Hill, where they make a well loved landmark for all Brighton's visitors.

However, before either of them were to appear, another post mill stood at the same spot. It had been there since 1765 and was known as Duncton or Dungate mill. Equipped with two sets of stones, it was capable of grinding sufficient flour to fill 700 sacks a week (each sack weighing one cwt) and was by all accounts an extremely successful enterprise. As such it continued until approximately 1853 when the owner, a Mr Mitchell, (no relation to the blacksmith) seeking to capitalise on the situation, seized the opportunity to purchase a second post mill (Jill) that owing to an impending railway cutting, was being taken down on the hills near Dyke Road.

Jack and Jill windmills, Clayton – showing the stump of the original Duncton or Dungate mill in the foreground

About this, R. Thurston Hopkins says:

> The small mill (the post mill) called Jill was built by Mr Lashmar in Dyke Road, Brighton in 1821. It stood above the railway tunnel, but was afterwards moved to Clayton. At first it was attempted to move it with horses, but the spasmodic jerking on the ropes caused them to snap so often, that oxen were employed to finish the job. Oxen pull with a steady and even power, and are admirably suited to such work.

It is thought that between fifty and eighty of these animals were engaged in the task, and what a stirring sight it must have been to watch the huge beasts patiently hauling the great timbers of the dismantled mill on that long dusty road to Clayton.

So in due course Jill was erected to the west of the existing mill and both operated profitably for a time, until that is, it became evident that the venerable Duncton was rapidly deteriorating with age. Because of its poor condition, the 'old fellow' was demolished, leaving just the roundhouse, and a modern tower mill (Jack) was constructed immediately alongside, with a connecting door between. It is said that 100,000 bricks were used for the purpose, making it proof against the wildest storm. There were four circular floors, each decreasing in size, and from the uppermost, a ladder led up to a sort of enclosed crow's nest in the cap.

Following Mr Mitchell's death, a Mr Hammond and his son acquired the lease. In order to improve working conditions and to lessen the chance of spoiling the flour by unnecessary exposure to weather, they created a dry walkway between Jack and the granary by connecting the two with a tunnel.

In 1903, the mills changed hands yet again when a Mr Wood, the last man to work them took on the business. In his book *A Sussex Farmer,* he mentions the tunnel:

> One of my men who had been there many years told me that on rough days, before the tunnel was made, he could only get from his house to the mill, or from the mill to his house, by lying flat on the ground and crawling across the open space, it was impossible to stand upright. When he first went there, he told me that in his ignorance he started to keep chickens, but gave it up when he had lost most of them, blown bodily away into Clayton Village several hundred feet below.

Mr Wood employed a miller and a carter, and both men with their respective families lived in adjoining cottages on the premises. The following extract which was taken from a letter written by a Mr D. Wooller (the carter's grandson) reveals the briefest glimpse of what life must have been like in those far off days:

> My grandfather, Mr R. Wooller, was the carter. He made a daily trip to Brighton with his cart and a team of six horses to deliver the flour to various places. On his return he would call at the forge at Patcham to have the horses shod. On the last part of the trip my grandfather would sleep and allow the horses to find their own way home. My grandfather lived at the mills for several years and seven of his eight children were born there, including my father. The only means of transport was walking and the route taken for a trip to the Matsfield Arms, or for shopping and the daily trip to school, was down the side of the hill and through the farm at the bottom. During the winter they would cut a footpath through the snow, leaving the shovel at the bottom of the hill for the return journey. If the snow was to drift into the road leading to the mill, the cart would be taken over the fields and into the main road.

The working life of the mills was now almost at an end, and by 1908 it had ceased altogether. Mr Edward Martin, the author of *Sussex Geology and other Essays* used them as a base for a short period while he conducted a study of downland dewponds, and then in 1911, they were purchased by Captain Anson R.N.(retired) who took up residence with his wife. The Captain died soon after the end of the First World War, but Mrs Anson and a lady companion, Miss Jones, continued to live there for several years. A little of the Ansons' somewhat eccentric background is revealed by Henry Longhurst, the golfing correspondent and writer, who during the early 1950s, also became the owner of the mills. In his entertaining autobiography, *My Life and Soft Times*, he describes his first visit to the premises:

> We were taken round by Miss Jones, an elderly Victorian lady, passing from one tiny dark room to another, many with names like the Captain's Cabin, Mrs Anson's room, the Parlour, and so on. An underground passage ran from the granary to some steps leading up to the ground floor of Jack and from here one passed through to the stump of a third and much older mill called Duncton, a single round room in which you could almost feel the peace and hear the silence. In a glass case on the wall were a red and gold baton and some ancient medals, and it was these which led us round to the history of the place. The medals, it seemed, had been struck for the great Admiral Anson on the occasion of his victory off Finisterre in 1747. The baton was the 'Gold Stick' carried by his descendant, Captain Anson RN at the coronation of George V. This Captain Anson had an overwhelming desire to retire to a lighthouse but, none appearing to be available, he did the next best thing and determined to 'civilise' the then deserted windmill, Jack, which would still as a matter of fact, make a perfect lighthouse."

A team of farm horses descending Clayton Hill

Having acquainted ourselves with the mills and their history, we return once more to the road. A glance at its excellent surface makes it hard to believe that as recently as 1922, the condition was so poor that it was a route to be avoided if at all possible, especially during the winter months. Complaints about its dangerous state were so many and so vociferous, that a group of businessmen with an eye for an investment, formed a consortium and put it to the authorities that the time had come for a new and modern road to be laid over the Downs at this point. Their overtures were clearly persuasive for a meeting was held at the Brighton Royal Pavilion to discuss the matter in greater detail. The *Mid Sussex Times* reported the proceedings in full, and some of the arguments supporting the proposal are condensed in the following extract:

> At a meeting held at the Brighton Royal Pavilion a Mr T. H. Scutt C.E. stated that in place of the present crooked road, one should be constructed of sufficient width to enable two cars going north and two going south to pass with ample space on either side. He had a friend at Ditchling who travelled six miles instead of two in order to reach Pyecombe so that he would avoid the hill. The hill – however charming the view – had been a burden for generations, it was a great drawback to agriculture because in slippery weather it took horses two or three hours to surmount it. In many instances farmers sent their horses all the way round Hurstpierpoint so as to escape the hill. Was something to be done, or were they going to wait until some pleasure excursionists ventured down the hill, the brakes gave out and probably the whole of the passengers were hurled into eternity?

Despite such forebodings, his audience remained unconvinced, and to the presumed chagrin of the gentleman from Ditchling, not to mention the farmers, nothing changed and the hill remained a formidable obstacle to both motorised and horse-drawn traffic alike.

Forging an unlikely link between the problems thus encountered, and of all things – the art of cookery! was an unhygienic tip contained in a memoir of childhood published by the *Hassocks Talk About* magazine, in which the contributor, a lady who had lived at Clayton in the years preceding the First World War, had this to say:

> .....when the carrier was at the top of Clayton Hill, he would blow his horn to indicate his arrival. He would put the skidpans under the rear wheels of the coach to descend the hill, and upon arrival at the Matsfield Arms, the shopkeeper would be waiting for him with a slice of bacon, which the carrier promptly placed onto the extremely hot skidpan and proceeded to cook his breakfast.

Coming down from the junction with Mill Lane, the road bends to the right, and on the western side there used to be a huge chalk pit that over the years has been filled with rubbish, a place it is said, where a number of damaged military vehicles were buried during the course of the Second World War. Many years prior to that, indeed, prior to the turn of the century, it was the site of the Clayton (or as some say) Pyecombe, lime-quarries. This was a thriving industry in its day, but one with a slightly sinister reputation, for during inclement weather, the warmth and dryness of the kilns would attract tramps and vagrants seeking shelter. And in many cases, the poor wretches, unaware of the poisonous nature of the fumes and probably congratulating themselves on having found a cosy billet, fell asleep – never to wake again.

Just north of the quarries stood a bungalow by the name of 'Selah'. The word is biblical in origin, and according to *A Dictionary of the Bible* is a musical or liturgical sign, indicating a pause and although rather an unusual title for a property, it was obviously considered appropriate by the original occupier. This gentleman, the late James Craig, as well as being an eminent man of letters and an authority on hymnology, was also the editor of a number of well known religious publications, such as *Great Thoughts* and *The Christian Age*. During a long and distinguished journalistic career, which included fifty-six years in Fleet Street, it was said of him that he could recall the days when copy was brought from the Houses of Parliament on horseback!

Having unlimited missionary zeal, he decided upon reaching retirement, to devote the rest of his life to the saving of souls. Initially this entailed a lot of work and no little expense, as he converted a barn on his land into what was to become known as 'The Barn

The Old Barn Meeting House

Mission Chapel', or the 'Old Barn Meeting House'. He fitted the interior with a pedal-organ and enough seating to accommodate a congregation, and when all was ready, held services there every Sunday. The venture was well supported from the beginning, with some worshippers prepared to walk all the way from Hurstpierpoint to 'hear the word of the Lord'. And not just 'the word' as it happened, for the more hardy amongst their number were baptised as well. Dressed in white robes, the supplicants were ceremoniously lowered into a large water filled tank, and then hauled out again drenched to the skin. Mr Craig who quite evidently was not a believer in half-measures, made sure they had been completely immersed.

One would search in vain for the establishment now, because it was destroyed by fire many years ago. The bungalow too has gone, a new property standing in its place, and all that is left to remind one of Mr Craig and his good intentions, is a house with a curious name.

We have now descended to Clayton, a beautiful spot that consists of a church, the remains of a farmyard, some pleasant dwellings and little else. Much of the parish lies on what is known as 'gault', which is a bed of clay and marl (a rich fertilising earth). So the name of the area almost certainly originates from the expression, 'Claeg Tun', which means 'Clay Farmstead'. The *Domesday Book* refers to it as 'Claitune'. Later it became known as 'Claetona', and eventually became the 'Clayton' we know today.

The little village church of St John the Baptist is Saxon in origin and is also mentioned in the *Domesday Book*, while its chancel arch and nave (which bears wall paintings of considerable antiquity) are said to date back to the reign of Edward the Confessor, or possibly even earlier.

In keeping with the age of the building, the three church bells are some of the oldest to be found in Sussex. The first of these, dated 1420, was cast by Richard Hill of London. The second, which is nearly as ancient, has the rare cross-keys marking, while the third, a comparative newcomer to the assembly, was cast by Samuel Knight in 1713.

The consecration of Clayton Churchyard Extension by the Bishop of Chichester, Dr G. K .A. Bell, in 1940. Leading the procession are the churchwardens, George Allwood (left, front) and Mr W. B. Adams

Foot of Clayton Hill looking south. The lime quarries can be seen to the right of the road

Clayton Farm. The pond is now filled in, while the barn and outbuildings have been converted to dwellings

The village however is far older than its church and as with Pyecombe on the other side of the hill, probably boasted a community before the existence of Rome. Speaking of which, in his book *Downland Pathways*, A. Hadrian Allcroft refers to evidence of some Roman remains in the district, he states that the substructure of a villa, some mosaic flooring and a bath lies buried in the garden of the former rectory. If right, it suggests that Clayton must have been a fairly important place at the time, for Mr Allcroft also believed that Underhill Lane was used by the Romans to link Streat and Westmeston with Coldharbour Corner near Wolstonbury, the point where the great Roman highway from London swung westwards towards Portslade.

A view of Clayton from the Downs, taken before the graveyard was extended at the rear of the Church

The Burgess Hill Waterworks Pumping Station at Clayton

Proof that the sterling qualities of the Roman colonists could still be found in the village was amply demonstrated when, after the outbreak of the Second World War, seven men from this tiny community stood on guard on the South Downs, waiting with shotguns and pitchforks to stem Hitler's mechanised hordes should they land a few miles away on Brighton beach. Known as the L.D.V. (Local Defence Volunteers) these seven men of Clayton formed their own little army on the occasion that Anthony Eden made his call to arms. With neither uniform nor equipment, and identified only by white handkerchiefs tied about their arms, they patrolled the hills every night, keeping a vigilant watch for the Hun. The late Mr H. E. Cooper said:

> We heard the roar of the German coastal batteries as our planes went over – and then looked at our shotguns and pitchforks! One lady (Mrs Anson from the Windmills) heard we had not enough shotguns to go round, and came out with an old rook rifle and half a dozen rounds of ammunition – we were glad of it.

By September 1940, the L.D.V. had been renamed the Home Guard, and the Clayton section, now kitted out with uniforms and rifles, was practising physical training and stalking three or four times a week. Their orders came from the company commander at Keymer, but the members themselves remained fiercely democratic, and for a while at least, each man refused to accept a position above his comrades. Their burning ambition according to Mr Cooper, was quite simply:

> To bring down a raider with rifle fire. When we do that, much ale will be drunk at the Village Inn.

Fortunately for the Luftwaffe, it was not destined to happen, but somehow the press got hold of the story, and both the *Evening Standard* and the *Evening News* published articles concerning the Clayton warriors. The *News* described them as "seven men whose spirit Hitler will never break in a thousand years of Blitzkrieg."

They are all gone now and we must go too, but surely not before saluting the memories of Edward Cooper (coal merchant), Fred Eastwood (Greengrocer), Bill Small (Gravedigger), Captain Barlow (Civil Engineer), George Allwood (Nurseryman), Hesketh Lodge (Motor Mechanic) and Harry Leighton (Chauffeur).

At the junction of Underhill Lane there is a view of the fortified entrance to Clayton Tunnel with its little cottage (formerly the residence of the tunnel keeper) situated snugly between the turrets.

Immediately below this uniquely positioned premises is an imposing if somewhat sinister Gothic archway built in Caen stone and white brick through which the track disappears into impenetrable blackness. Constructed in the early 1840s at the then considerable cost of £90,000 this fine example of Victorian engineering is 2266 yards long, 270 feet below ground at its deepest point, and has remained in continuous use since it first opened over 150 years ago. Then of course 'steam was king', and in order to disperse the suffocating smoke that it was anticipated would collect in such a confined space, a number of huge shafts were bored down from the surface to provide ventilation. In consequence, the precise route of the underground passage may be easily traced by simply following the line of gigantic chimney pots that straddle the hill between the two entrances.

Trains of the period were of course much slower than they are now, and the carriages were unlit, which meant that the journey beneath the Downs would have been spent in total darkness. Therefore to avoid any possible unease on the part of their customers, the Directors of the Railway Company decided to install gas lighting in the tunnel. This they felt sure would calm the most timid of souls – indeed, to say that they had passed gas-lit through the bowels of the earth would give passengers something to brag about, surely that would be worth the price of the ticket alone? So the company had a gasworks built close to Hassocks Gate Station, where the commodity was manufactured and piped to a series of naked flares with fish tail burners that had been fitted onto the white painted walls of the tunnel. For a while all went well, the application of what was then, very advanced technology, greatly impressed the travelling public. But rather ironically, it was an advance in a different technology that ultimately led to its downfall. For as the design of rail stock improved, its speed increased, with the result that the tremendous draughts created kept extinguishing the flares. Despite their best endeavours it was a problem that the company was unable to resolve, and so the gas light went out – and stayed out!

Clayton Tunnel – in the age of steam!

In 1861, the tunnel gained much unwanted publicity from its being the scene of the most terrible accident that had yet occurred in railway history. Two trains collided in inky darkness with horrific results. Twenty-five people perished, a further 176 were injured, and grisly descriptions of the carnage received a national press coverage that lasted for several weeks. What was to become known as the Clayton Tunnel Disaster was reported round the world.

This dreadful event has been described by numerous people on many occasions, and several suggestions have been volunteered as to why it happened. But few accounts are more concise than that which appeared in the *Hassocks Talk About* in October 1977. It stated:

> Clayton Tunnel was flanked by signal boxes at either end which were connected by a single needle telegraph, and the London Brighton and South Coast Railway Company instructions were that only one train should be in the tunnel at any one time.
>
> Early on the morning in question, two excursion trains were due to leave Brighton for London as well as the usual stopping trains. The first train which had come from Portsmouth, was late arriving along the south coast line and the assistant station-master at Brighton was very concerned that his schedules were being delayed. Eventually the Portsmouth excursion was dispatched from Brighton at 8.28am, about 30 minutes late. The Brighton excursion which had been held up by the delay was sent off very quickly after it at 8.31am followed by the Brighton Parliamentary (stopping train) at 8.35am.
>
> At Clayton Tunnel, Henry Killick was on duty in his signal box at the southern end. As the first train, the Portsmouth excursion, steamed into Pyecombe cutting, all was in order. The train passed the signal box and went into the tunnel, but Killick immediately saw that the trip-signal had failed to operate. He was attempting to set the signal to stop when he saw another train coming up the line. There was no time to set the signal and in desperation he thrust his red flag out of the signal box just as the engine went by. To his dismay the engine steamed into the tunnel and the second train disappeared from sight.
>
> Killick checked that the signal was now set to stop and telegraphed the signalman John Brown at the Clayton end of the tunnel. Using Morse code he sent "Is the train out?"
>
> At that moment John Brown was watching the Portsmouth excursion rattle past his box and he gave back the answer "Yes."
>
> To be quite sure, Killick again signalled "Is the train out?" and once more Brown telegraphed "Yes."
>
> Henry Killick set his signal to 'All Clear', and the third train which had by now arrived at Pyecombe cutting, steamed into the tunnel at 40mph.
>
> Inside the tunnel, the driver of the second train who had seen the red flag thrust out of the signal box brought his engine to a halt, and was reversing the train back to the tunnel's entrance when with just 300 yards to go, the terrible collision occurred. The engine of the Brighton Parliamentary completely demolished the rear coach of the excursion train, and came to rest on the remains of the next coach up, spilling hot coals from the fire box and scalding water from its boiler in the process.

The horror of the scene hardly bears contemplating, especially when considering how long the passengers were trapped. When assistance eventually came, several hours had gone by. A doctor and some villagers walked over the hill from Hassocks Gate and on receipt of the news the authorities sent help from Brighton, but it was not until the end of the day that the magnitude of the disaster was fully realised.

For dispatching the three trains in such rapid succession, an act that was clearly contrary to the rules of the company – not to mention common sense, the assistant station master of Brighton was, during the inquest into the affair, accused of committing multiple manslaughter – a charge for which he was eventually acquitted, although he was to bear the odium for the rest of his life. No blame was apportioned to either Henry Killick or John Brown, however the shortcomings of the system could hardly be ignored, and we will learn later how the Clayton Tunnel disaster helped hasten the day

The excavation for the gas holder at Hassocks Gate Yard

when safety measures would be developed to ensure that a similar tragedy could never occur again.

After emerging from the tunnel, the railway track in its deep cutting passes virtually unnoticed under the road bridge as it heads, straight as an arrow, to the north. But the road twists and turns all the way to Stonepound and the traveller merely has to look and he will be rewarded with breathtaking views of the South Downs and the lovely countryside of the Weald. Everything blends to perfection here, even the public house known as the 'Jack and Jill' has its charms. This name however, although eminently suitable when considering the position, is not the one by which it was originally known. Local people who have reached a certain age, remember it better as the Matsfield Arms. A place with a curious history in so far that it has only functioned as a full time pub since 1939. Prior to that it had a six day licence and was at one and the same time, the village pub, the grocery store and the post office.

> Two penny stamps, a pound of rashers and a pint of bitter, please Fred.

That was the kind of order the landlord, Fred Kirby, received – and by the time the customer had consumed his ale, and perhaps tried for double top on the dartboard, the purchases all neatly wrapped, were waiting his collection.

In a sense it was the very popularity of the enterprise that proved to be its undoing at least as far as the wives of the village were concerned. Their husbands spent so much time and money 'shopping' at the Matsfield Stores, that the landlord discovering he could make more profit from beer than provisions, applied for and was granted a seven day licence in which to sell his brew. He then built an extension

The Matsfield Arms – a public house cum post office and grocer's shop

Coldharbour Farm, Clayton – with Bert Cherriman and Ernie Wakeford pitching sheaves onto the wagon

to the bar, and to the fury of the local women folk closed down the post office and shop to run a full time pub instead. At the time this bold man was quoted as saying:

> The village is very upset I know, but it can't be helped, we need the room. I shall have no time for selling stamps and bacon now.

And that as they say, was that.

Whether the same landlord held the licence in 1913 seems unlikely. But if such were the case, he might have well thought twice before upsetting the village wives, for in that year the feminine spirit was on the move, as was amply demonstrated by a procession of extremely doughty and determined women who passed within a 'stone's throw' of his doorstep as they made their way to London.

They were members of the Suffragist Society and the purpose of the pilgrimage was to unite with thousands of others who were taking part in similar protest marches throughout the country. Their colours – green, white and scarlet were freely worn, banners were carried, one lady had a drum, another a violin and as they marched they sang:

A good heart and a steady mind,
Our purpose clear in view,
And we will show our country now
What women folk can do.
From Land's End by the blue sea coast,
From far beyond the Tweed.
We march that all our countryside
May know the women's need.

Chorus

And shall they scorn the women's voice
When we for justice cry?
We're marching in our thousands now
To know the reason why.

Processions had set off from every point of the compass and like tributaries, joined together, increased in size, and upon reaching the capital, surged into Hyde Park to be addressed in rousing terms by their leaders. And the unmistakeable message from the assembly was that the women of England not only demanded the right to vote, but intended to pursue this claim by all lawful means at their disposal.

It was planned that the Sussex contingent would proceed northwards from Brighton and travelling at approximately 3 miles per hour or ten miles per day, go via Clayton and Burgess Hill and then on to Cuckfield, Handcross and Crawley, with rallies held on the way. Those who wished to be associated with the cause, but were unable to complete the full distance registered their support by either cycling or walking alongside the pilgrims for as long as they felt able.

Mrs Ivy Dudeney, who was a girl of sixteen at the time, could clearly remember the march, and was present when the suffragettes halted at Burgess Hill to hold a meeting beneath the well known gospel tree.

> " A large crowd had gathered," she recalled. "It was fairly good natured, but most of those there regarded the women as cranks (a lot of people did in those days) so they shouted and made jokes at nearly everything that was said, even the policeman on duty was laughing. I laughed as well, it seemed the right thing to do at the time, but deep down I felt slightly ashamed."

From a postcard of the period

The Suffragist march to London, passing through Clayton – July 1913

A short distance from the Jack and Jill pub, the road rises to the crest of a hill, and a glance to the east reveals a small cattle bridge that crosses the railway line. Known to local folk as Misty Bridge, it is worthy of mention if for no other reason than its parapets are inscribed with the still legible initials of some Canadian servicemen who in the build up preceding the D-Day landings, were encamped in the nearby woods. One such legend reads:

Bill Brunton
P.P.C.L.I.*
8 July 1942
Sioux Lookout
Ontario
Canada

In 1986, Mr L. A. Rawlins, a Hassocks resident who for many years had been intrigued by this particular inscription, wrote to City Hall at Sioux Lookout, enquiring whether Mr Brunton was still known in the area. He was, and Mr Rawlins received a reply: an extract from which is given here:

> I know now for sure where I was July 8/42 wouldn't you say? I spent a lot of time in Sussex the first three years before going to the Italian Campaign – one of the D-Day dodgers as Lady Astor called us. Being a Dispatch Rider, most of the time I had a motor cycle issued to me, so was able to get around quite easily and certainly burned up a lot of gas. Guess I had a habit of carving my name and address wherever I went, never thinking it would finally catch up with me.
>
> Thanks for writing – at least someone knows I was there!

Our allies, tall and cheerful in their smart uniforms were made to feel welcome in the neighbourhood and deservedly so, for the majority of them were courteous, friendly and most important of all as far as the village traders were concerned – free with their money. An excellent combination and one that not surprisingly, the local girls (whose boyfriends were far away) found irresistible, which was good news for the visitors but not for the unfortunate absentees.

The darker side of the men's character was rarely revealed, although there were occasional stories of drunken violence and fearful knife fights in of all places, the respectable streets of Hurstpierpoint. Such incidents however were infrequent and swiftly dealt with by the military authorities who had total responsibility in these matters.

And as if cheerfulness, availability and unlimited money were not enough, during the particularly severe winters of those years, our visitors displayed an incredible talent for skating, as the recollections of Tom Hedgecock, a former resident of the village clearly reveal:

> "I was only a boy at the time," he said. "But it seemed as if the soldiers could skate as easily as I could walk, and when the pond at Belmont froze over, you couldn't keep them away.They loved to show off in front of the girls, and the girls had a go too, except they weren't so good, which wasn't surprising considering they'd got no skates. They just staggered about and kept falling over, but to judge by the squealing and laughing, it was obvious they didn't mind too much. The blokes really were good though and did a lot of fancy stuff. The blackout regulations might not have existed for all they cared, when it got dark, they just lit hurricane lamps and carried on skating. One of them was playing an accordion as he twirled about. It was lovely to listen to the music and watch the lights weave around in the dark, even though I fully expected to hear the warden's whistle any minute. He must have been aware, so must half of Hassocks come to that. I think he was keeping his head down, those Canadians were a pretty tough bunch. Friendly though, and generous, I'll never forget them."

*- *PPCLI stands for Princess Patricia's Canadian Light Infantry.*

Allwood Bros.

Childhood Days ~ The Founding of the Firm ~ Clayton Nursery

On the eastern side of the road as it rises to Stonepound, is a derelict nursery — all that remains of the Clayton branch of Allwood Brothers, the world famous carnation specialists. Now it is just a ghost town of rickety glasshouses laid to siege by brambles, thistles and scrub.

The state of the ruins, the neglect and decay, makes it hard to believe that at one time they were a hive of activity, and that the company was easily the largest employer of labour in the district, drawing its workforce from Hassocks, Hurstpierpoint, Burgess Hill and even Brighton.

Yet such was the case, and the history of the brothers concerned – Edward, Montagu and George Allwood – deserves recording, not only for its interest, but because it is a classic example of the triumph of will over adversity. Their rapid rise to success as growers and breeders of carnations was entirely as a result of belief in themselves, belief in their product, and an infinite capacity to work. They founded the firm in 1910 at Wivelsfield Green, as Montagu states in his book, *The Third and Fourth Generation,*

> with much confidence and little capital.

This determination to succeed was undoubtedly engrained in their character during a childhood spent at Grange Farm, their parents' home at Ludford Magna in the Lincolnshire wolds. There were nine children, four boys and five girls, and they received a typical Victorian upbringing in which the virtues of honesty, duty, and self-reliance played an all-important role. The times however were difficult for farmers, and particularly so for their father, whose bad luck and poor judgement led him to make a number of decisions that resulted in the family resources being squeezed to the limit, and with each passing year, the future became more uncertain.

By the time that Montagu had arrived – fourth on the list in 1879 – the point of no return had been passed. Life at Grange Farm was hard. Money was short, and the prospects very dark.

Sheep were Mr Allwood senior's pride, and sheep it would seem were his downfall, or at least they were one of the reasons. He had 1,000 Lincolnshire long-woolled sheep, as large as donkeys (and about as edible!) with wool that was extremely coarse. Not surprisingly, such animals attracted little commercial demand, and the income they produced was negligible. Hoping vainly for an upturn in fortune, he persisted with them, only to see his little capital continue to shrink until it reached the point where he could carry on no longer. The end when it came, in 1893, is touchingly described by Montagu:

> There is positive pain in this ending of the old life, and its associations, even for a small boy of fourteen. The furniture is sold on the lawn; once it looked so choice and good, now it looks so poor and mean. But you, and a precious few, are the only ones who want these worldly goods to look valuable; practically everything the family possesses is sold because you are moving into a small house in the street of a town. These things impress children who for years had realised the struggle their parents had put up against hard times and misfortunes. The small economies, such as stopping the daily paper; the passing of the sirloin of beef and the appearance of the rougher joints on the table; the dismissal of stable boy and maids – these are incidents that are remembered. When the market town had to be visited, sandwiches were taken for economy's sake, buns took the place of cake; everything was done to make money, while economy in every detail was studied to save money. And always lingered the hope for a turn in the tide and the return of prosperity to agriculture.
>
> But at last tragedy came, and between her sobs, Mother told us that Father had to give up the Grange Farm. There was to be a sale to try and pay his debts, and Mother did not know where we should go and live. So our castle which seemed so large, so big and so strong, figuratively fell to

Commemorative run of the London to Brighton coach in the 1930s – passing Clayton nursery

> the ground, and everyone who could earn anything had to commence work. Thus all was broken up and our family was scattered.

One can understand Mrs Allwood's tears, for those were the days before social security existed and only the workhouse stood between the dispossessed and the gutter, therefore their situation must have seemed desperate indeed. But if such thoughts were on her mind, then she had not reckoned on the strong and steady character that she and her husband had bequeathed their sons. As far as they were concerned, it was a case of 'all hands to the pumps' and so the boys sought and gained employment, Edward with a seed merchant and Montagu on a nursery, with George gaining a similar position as soon as he was of age. And the fact that they worked hard and succeeded in their chosen careers is borne out by the following extract from Montagu's book:

> Prior to entering our great enterprise, Edward had climbed high in the seed trade, also as a maltster and judge of grain, while George, with varied horticultural experience, had developed into a highly skilled grower. I had built up the Carnation Department of the firm I was with, invented and introduced new lines, written a book, compounded a fertilizer, and helped in general management.

This then was the brothers' background and the foundation on which they were to build their company. The idea of going it alone had been on their minds for some time, but had never developed beyond the initial discussion stage. The pieces all fell into place in 1908 when George, who had been working in nursery management in the USA, returned to this country to attend his sister's wedding. While over here, he told his brothers of the way carnations were being grown more profitably in America, and what he said impressed them so much, that they decided this was the idea they had been waiting for, and proposed there and then to set up a firm in England to be run on similar lines. The fact that their joint savings amounted to less than £500 in no way dissuaded them: they were three bachelors and would live on bread and cheese if necessary, so sure were they of the ultimate success of their scheme. Robert Allwood (George's son) now takes up the story:

> The key to the plan was that Edward and Montagu were to look for a small nursery to rent, that would not only bring in an early income, but had sufficient land alongside that they could purchase, thus enabling them to build greenhouses to the new design. This they were to eventually find at Wivelsfield Green.

> Then in 1910, my father came back from the USA to start up the nursery. He brought with him some newer American varieties to add to Montagu's breeding stock, and then arranged the building of the first greenhouse, which at the time was the largest single span construction of the sort in the country.

This greenhouse, which was completed in 1911, created quite a sensation and provided the fledgling company with some excellent publicity, more of which was gained the following year, when the newly established Allwood Brothers trounced its English rivals for honours at the International Horticultural Shows. In the short space of a couple of years, this little pipsqueak company from Sussex had gained the respect of carnation growers throughout the world. This respect increased in 1913 when the firm successfully bred its highly popular perpetual flowering carnation 'Mary Allwood'.

All this dramatic progress came to an abrupt end with the outbreak of war in 1914. First Edward and then George volunteered, as did most of their staff who were fit for military service. Girls were engaged in their place and carnation growing was curtailed for the duration. The company concentrated instead on producing food – onions, potatoes and beans etc.

They were testing times for all concerned, for those in uniform, and those left behind. Montagu, who had remained to watch over the firm, felt the strain of their parting enormously, and like everyone else, lived in constant fear of the arrival of the dreaded telegram! Many years later he was to express that concern most vividly:

> He [Edward] had just finished telling me of one of his experiences as a Dispatch Rider; how he had to take a

dispatch through a long dark wood, when the Germans were advancing, and had pushed forward their scouts to ascertain the lie of the land.

Crouched low over the handlebars, and going all out, some bullets seemed to pass unpleasantly near; at last one seemed to strike his knee, also to pierce the petrol tank. Fearing the worst, he dared not look down, but steadied himself to push on until he dropped or the motor cycle stopped. At last, having got clear of the wood, and outdistanced the enemy, he found that neither was he injured, nor the machine damaged. Either a spent bullet, or a stone or a cake of mud had struck his knee. So all was well and he could carry on.

Incidents such as this, and extraordinary escapes, were almost daily experiences in the fighting line; they taught us, as brothers, that the most slender thread alone held us together. If it had snapped all our desires and dreams would have come to an end; gone would have been our prospects, and all on which we had built such brave and high hopes.

Montagu need not have feared, for Edward and George survived unscathed, and upon their return the company reverted once more to carnation production, and welcomed back its employees to the posts that had been kept open for them. All was to be as before, with one exception. Edward, although retaining a stake in the company, was content to let his more horticulturally-minded brothers run the day - to-day business, while he returned to farming in Lincolnshire.

Again the firm prospered, one of the main reasons being, the unprecedented success that Montagu had in hybridising the old garden fringed white pink with the greenhouse perpetual flowering carnation. This new race of plants was named *Dianthus Allwoodii* by the scientific committee of the Royal Horticultural Society and in Montagu's book he says

The success of this plant was instantaneous. The situation was such indeed, that we were confronted with the necessity of building new greenhouses, and taking over a branch nursery, and even then for years we were unable to cope with the demand."

Rapid expansion became necessary, the brothers first rented a premises at Plumpton, then a little later acquired the lease to Clayton with the option to buy, which they did in 1922. This proved to be convenient because a terrace of three cottages fronted onto the site, so George, who was about to be married, moved into one, his foreman went into another, and the third was rented out.

The Clayton branch was situated on a four-acre site and contained several greenhouses, a number of sheds, a stable block and an antiquated watering system that was reliant on a wind-driven pump, none of which was remotely suitable for the growing of carnations! To convert such a place without involving colossal cost and considerable time would have taxed the ingenuity of most nurserymen, but not apparently George Allwood. He after all had already built the largest greenhouse in England, and what he had done before, he could do again, and did.

Pulling down several of the smaller houses, he used their timber and glass to construct a huge 'ridge and furrow' type greenhouse, after which he dismantled, enlarged and then re-erected many of the other original houses. Tackling the inadequacies of the existing water supply proved to be more difficult, but after a period of experimentation that included the drilling of two separate wells, and the installation of a 40-foot high watertower, the situation was finally resolved to his satisfaction.

Despite the general depression, there can be little doubt that the 1920s and the 1930s were the hey-day of the company, as Robert Allwood in his family history points out:

Between the wars, new greenhouses of the ridge and furrow type were erected almost yearly at Clayton, so more land at the back of the nursery was purchased from the Danny estate, and eventually the entire field was acquired. Another field between the nursery and Stone Pound (the site of the present Garden Centre) was also taken over, this had much lighter soil and was ideal for growing pinks. In addition, we rented yet more land on the old spoil-heaps of the then disused sand pits which were just across the road.

During that same time, a new race of Hardy Perpetual Border Carnations had been raised at Wivelsfield, as well as a race of Rock Dianthus with the Alpine species as mother parents – and Montagu Allwood's book *Carnations and All Dianthus*, first published in 1926 (and still regarded by many to be the definitive work on the subject) accorded its author and the company with the reputation of being the finest breeders and growers of carnations and related species in the world.

However, history was about to repeat itself, for in 1939 just as it had in 1914, the nursery was required to switch its output from the production of carnations to the production of food – mainly tomatoes and lettuce. And George Allwood enlisted once again, but this time into the Local Defence Volunteers (later to be re-named the Home Guard) where he was eventually promoted to the rank of Lance Corporal. The younger men also enlisted, and as happened before,women were engaged in their place, and a cosmopolitan crowd they were too, for their numbers not only included local girls who did their war service on the nursery, but also some young ladies who had been evacuated from the Black Cat cigarette factory in London.

At the end of the conflict in 1945, life slowly returned to normal but it was a different world and things would never be the same again. Having enjoyed just a few short years of the peace, Bill Pointing, the foreman of the Clayton nursery, an employee who had been with George from the outset, died quite unexpectedly. And it would seem as if the position was jinxed, for his successor, George Russell (one of whose claims to fame was that he had been born in the cottage over Clayton Tunnel) hardly lived long enough to savour the fruits of promotion, before he too expired without warning.

Despite such tragic losses, the business continued to thrive under George's and Montagu's stewardship, but they were no longer young men. It was during these twilight years that one of the co-authors of this book worked for a while at Clayton, and the brief and affectionate portrayal of George Allwood that follows, is taken from

Montagu Allwood

Edward Allwood, James Allwood, George Allwood and Robert Allwood at Clayton Nursery in 1935

George Allwood and the staff of Clayton Nursery during the Second World War

his unpublished memoirs of the period:

> George Allwood was in the nicest sense, a character. In appearance he reminded me greatly of the famous American film director Cecil B. de Mille. He was a director too in his way, and with twinkling eyes and jaunty step, would walk the daily round of his own particular set, checking that everything was just so, and when in a good mood, gave warning of his approach by whistling a catchy little tune. And while he could be awkward on occasion, he also possessed the priceless ability to laugh at himself. I well recall an instance when he failed to duck and in consequence stuck his head against a beam. It was a painful blow and gingerly rubbing the tender spot, he ruefully exclaimed "Not to worry, my head's like my name – Allwood"!

Edward, the eldest of the brothers died in 1956, and lies buried in Lincolnshire, the county of his birth. He was closely followed by Montagu who passed on in 1958 and his remains are interred in the pretty churchyard at Wivelsfield. George, who survived them both, died and was cremated at Grimsby in 1964. He and his wife are commemorated by a stone tablet set in the wall of the churchyard path at Clayton. Its simple inscription reads:

In memory of
George Wells Allwood
1881-1964
Nurseryman and churchwarden
and his wife
Jessie Helen
1887-1973
who both loved this church.

Catalogue illustration by Mark Dudeney, 1953

Hassocks

Hudson Sand Pit ~ The Roman Burial Ground ~ The Weald Tennis Club ~ Hassocks Scouts

The disused sand pits mentioned earlier by Robert Allwood were just across the road from his father's nursery. They had been excavated by the Hudson company, a concern that at the height of its production was a major supplier of sand to builder's merchants throughout the south of England. Because it was such a profitable operation, a spur line from Hassocks railway station was specially constructed to transport the sand directly from the quarry. The late Cyril Charman, a life-long resident, and a reliable authority on the area, refers to this line in an article that appeared in the *Hassocks and Keymer Talk About*:

> I do not know the date the line was laid, but it was probably before 1900. It was of course standard gauge and left the goods yard at a point opposite to where the goods office once stood. The motive power was supplied by the engine (usually one of the small tank variety) which came up from Brighton to shunt a number of open wagons to the point where the red sand was being excavated, then bring back the full ones that were put there previously. The number varied, but was usually six or nine, each wagon carrying a nine ton load. The bulk of the sand was dug out before 1914, but after that, the remains went to Hampden Park, Eastbourne, which had then started to develop, the Hassocks sand being highly thought of by the building trade.
>
> The line ran along the southern edge of the site that was to eventually become the Weald Lawn Tennis Club, passing under the A273 (Clayton Road) where the old cutting can still be seen just south of Stonepound Bus Stop. It was eventually closed when Messrs. Hudson's pit had advanced further westward, and they could not accept the price asked by the Railway Engineers Depot to extend the track."

Mr Charman might well have added that the Hudson company's enterprise yielded a lot more than building materials, for it was also a Romano-British burial ground, and it is a sad fact that many priceless archaeological artifacts were either damaged or destroyed because of the need to get the sand. Some precious articles (including a Roman chariot pin) found their way safely to The Barbican museum, but much that escaped destruction was spirited away by amateur collectors, local children, or anyone else who cared to visit the vicinity. The world and his neighbour appear to have had unlimited access to the site.

For instance: One lady recalled that when a girl, a daily walk for her was to follow the railway to the pits, where she used to pick up arrow heads and coins. And she has a nice Roman pot in her cabinet to this day! Another lady said:

> When we were children, my friend and I used these sandpits as our playground. We would make our way there by the tunnel under the road. The pits were the site of a Roman cemetery, and we often unearthed shards of Samian or other pottery, some of which I still have.

It would seem that her adventures came to a sudden end, for she went on to say:

> On one occasion, having entered the tunnel, we were trapped by a squeaky, grinding train that was slowly passing through, and had to press ourselves against the brickwork. We avoided it after that.

As has already been related, the spur line to the sand pits formed the southern boundary of the Weald Lawn Tennis Club. Before the existence of that association, the area was known as "The Hassocks", which quite simply means, rough tufts of grass. Not, on the face of it, a suitable surface for sporting activities, yet it was here that the Tennis Club found its home, and the courts were laid down in a setting which is as sheltered and picturesque as that of any club in the country.

The abandoned railway tunnel to Hudson Sand Pit

The choice of this position and the foundation of the Club, was as the result of the foresight and energy of one man – Percy Hill. It was he who saw the possibilities of the place: a piece of land well sheltered on the north by a steep bank, and on the south by a plantation of pine trees. The only possible drawback was the steam engine that might belch forth suffocating black smoke when passing by, and so stop play. But train or no train, the plans went ahead, and at a meeting on the 30th July, 1920, which was convened at the old Clayton Arms Park Hotel, and chaired by Lt. Col. W. R. Campion of Danny (the owner of the land) the club was formally constituted with Percy Hill as the Honorary Secretary.

Initially provision was made for two hard courts, five grass courts, and a croquet lawn. But the latter never materialised, and the ground allocated was eventually used for two more courts.

In October, horses and men from Mr Sidney Hole's farm at Albourne began carting 126 wagon loads of mould, which was the topsoil from Hudson's Sandpit, and spread it over the area before turfing. Then early in November, the job of cutting 13,000 downland turfs began at Wolstonbury. They were carted straight away and relaid at the Weald, the work being completed by the end of the month.

The Clubhouse was the last major purchase and this was a prefabricated building that had formerly served as sleeping quarters for officers of the Royal Corps of Signals who were based at Maresfield.

There was no grand opening. Percy Hill asked a few friends down for a game over Christmas, and that was it – the Club had started.

In the official history of what is now known as The Weald Lawn Tennis and Squash Rackets Club, the author Derrick Ayton, referring to the correspondence of those early days, mentions a letter sent by a gentleman from Ditchling. "One," Mr Ayton says, "that anyone who has served on a tennis club committee will recognise."

> Dear Hill,
> I thought you quite understood that in the event of a certain Burgess Hill individual being on the Committee of the Club, I automatically went off. Please wipe my name from the list of Committee men and oblige.

Despite such teething troubles the Club got off to a fine start, as may be gathered by the following informative article that appeared in the *Hassocks and Keymer Talk About* in 1978. The contributor, Mr V. S. Hedges, who was at the time President of the Weald, wrote:

> In the summer of 1921, the newly laid courts stood up well to the hard wear, and particularly to the Open Tournament which became a yearly event until 1939. L. A. Godfree was the first winner of the Men's Singles, a Davis Cup player, he won the Men's Doubles at Wimbledon partnered by Randolph Lycett in 1923, and the Mixed with his wife (Miss Kitty McKane, a singles champion) in 1926. He also had the distinction of having served the first ball on the present Wimbledon Centre Court. In later years other notable winners include E. C. Peters (one of the few Englishmen ever to have beaten the great W. T. Tilden)

A tournament held at the Weald Lawn Tennis Club in the 1920s

> R. Miki, the Japanese Davis Cup player, J. M. Hunt and J. Sangliar, a prominently ranked French player of the late 1930's. The best known of the lady winners was undoubtedly Mrs King (Miss P. E. Mudford) who represented Great Britain in the Wightman Cup.

In 1933, F. R. Burrow, a distinguished Wimbledon referee in his day, and an author of several books on the game, had this to say about the Club:

> ...there is always some good play to be seen there. The surroundings are very picturesque, as a pine wood runs the whole length of one side of the seven courts, making not only a perfect background for players, but a paradise for picnickers in fine weather. Hassocks is, indeed, perhaps best described as a 'picnic' tournament, where the tennis is not taken too seriously, and is therefore more enjoyed than at some of the big meetings.

Percy Hill was also a great supporter of Scouting for Boys, and after the movement was founded in 1908, immediately formed a troop at Hassocks, providing a stable at the rear of Birnham, his home at South Bank, for a headquarters. Mr Cyril Charman, a former scout leader himself, referred to this in an article that appeared in the *Talk About* magazine:

> I knew Colonel Hill very well,and talked to him a lot. He always said that the Hassocks Troop was the first to be started in Sussex. Unfortunately they were slow off the mark in getting registered at HQ and were therefore known as the '3rd Brighton' for a short period. I believe they carried on until the beginning of the First World War, and from older acquaintances I have it that for a time at least some of them did guard duty on the railway at Wivelsfield, just in case there might be an attempt to blow it up!
>
> I understand there were about sixty scouts coming not only from Hassocks, but all of the villages around, some from Pyecombe, Newtimber and even Poynings! They had a band, and somewhere in the present scout band (1979) is one of the original bugles that was bequeathed to me when I was a scout – and it is still being used."

Percy Hill died in 1986 and in a full and eventful life, represented his county in tennis, golf and hockey. During the First World War he served in the Royal Artillery on the Western Front, then spent two years in India before returning to Europe for the end of the war and the Army of Occupation in Germany. Subsequently he continued in the Territorials, rising to the rank of Lt. Colonel, and was awarded the Territorial Decoration.

Lt. Colonel Percy Hill, R.A.

Members of Hassocks Scout Troop parading at South Bank in the years preceding the First World War (Percy Hill standing seventh in from the left). The drummer, Israel Avery, the only son of a well known Hassocks merchant of the same name, was to fall at the battle of the Somme in 1916

Stonepound Crossroads

Stone Pound crossroads ~ Turnpikes ~ Road surface ~ Druids ~ Buttinghill Hundred

From South Bank it is only a couple of strides to Stone Pound crossroads, and to look at this busy junction now, it is hard to believe that between the wars, a white-gloved RAC patrolman regularly stood in the centre of the road directing traffic, and courteously saluted all who passed – including the local pedestrians! Robert Allwood recalled that the man positioned himself within a circle of bricks, apparently believing that although some drivers might not hesitate to run him over, they would think twice before hitting the bricks!

There was a time when turnpike gates regulated the traffic at this point, in fact there were two such gates on our road, one at Stone Pound and other at Ansty. They were actually toll-gates which had been erected across the highway, and travellers who wished to continue with their journey had to pay for the privilege of doing so. These gates were under the control of the turnpike commissioners who leased them by auction for a year at a time, the proceeds being used to keep the roads under repair. To give an indication of the amount of money that was involved, one lease dated 21-7-1806, was to a Mr Edward Pitt of Cuckfield, and it covered the tolls of the Preston, Stone Pound and Ansty gates at a rent of £2,000 per annum. Rather strangely, the toll-keepers, or pikemen as they were called, do not appear to have been bound by any form of regulation, and in the matter of charges, were apparently allowed to take what they could get. Not surprisingly, such freedom often led to abuses of the system, which in turn earned the practitioners a somewhat dubious reputation.

The traveller had to be wary. If for instance he arrived at Ansty intending to proceed on to Brighton, it was best he said so, for the cost of passing through the gate included the cost of the Stone Pound and Patcham Gates as well. And this would be stated on the ticket. If he omitted to mention his destination, he would pay the same amount and the ticket issued would cover him for that gate only. The consequence of which was by the time he reached the coast he might well have paid three times the price of the journey.

In certain instances, tolls were charged according to the width of a vehicle's wheels, and at one time farmers were persuaded to fit wheels of six inches or more for which they paid a reduced charge of just one penny. This compared with twopence for ordinary sizes, and threepence for narrow wheeled conveyances. The idea was that the wider wheels of the wagons would smooth the surface of the highway for faster traffic.

Whether this was successful or not is unknown, but something had to be done, for the general condition of Sussex roads of the period was deplorable. This is borne out most amusingly in two extracts from *Old Sussex and her Diarists* by Arthur J. Rees. Referring to Dr John Burton – a Greek scholar and clergyman who made a journey into 'Sussex mud' in 1750, and later published an account of his travels entitled *Iter Sussexiense* – he quotes:

> We were carried in a Sussex cart or two-horse wagon, and while the driver on foot at our side, drove the horses with his whip and a sort of discordant bellowing, we like prisoners turned back to back, were tossed forward, jolted asunder and tumbled together. Oh! what a novel vehicle this is.

This is followed by the comment for which Dr Burton is chiefly remembered:

> Come now my friend, I will set before you a sort of problem in Aristotle's fashion: Why is it that the oxen, swine, the women and all other animals are so long legged in Sussex? May it be the difficulty of pulling the feet out of so much mud by the strength of the ankle, that the muscles get stretched as it were, and the bones lengthened?

Looking south from Stone Pound crossroads

Stone Pound crossroads. The house to the right,'Royston', was the childhood home of the former Royal Couturier, the late Sir Norman Hartnell

Over 130 years later in 1881, conditions had still not improved, as is shown by an extract taken from an editorial on the subject that appeared in the *Mid Sussex Times*. Referring to the main route across St John's Common (Burgess Hill) it said:

> On leaving the house of a gentleman in London Road, before taking half a dozen steps, we found ourselves "fixed" in mire and clay, and it was not without some considerable difficulty that we kept our boots on. A little further up the road, we found another wayfarer in a still worse plight, for he had been into a slough that had run over and into his high boots. It was dark between the distant lamps and impossible to pick one's way. Coming up to Park Road we found the climax; here was a 'soft' place where the Hudson's Furniture van and horses had to be reversed before it could be drawn out again, and we were informed by a credible witness that a lime wagon had also defied the efforts of the carter for three hours to extricate it from the same spot.

There is a well known story (although its accuracy is not vouchsafed) that a traveller on one such muddy Sussex road, saw a hat resting on the surface. Lifting it, he found a fellow traveller underneath and beneath him – his horse!

During the Autumn season of 1911, a passer-by at the crossroads would have witnessed something out of the ordinary: a scene more akin to Stonehenge than Stone Pound, the reason being that the Southdown Lodge of the Ancient Order of Druids watched by hundreds of spectators, had gathered to plant an oak sapling in honour of the coronation of King George V and Queen Mary.

After initially assembling at the Hassocks Hotel, members of the Lodge (no. 478) accompanied by visiting brethren, formed up in a procession, and headed by the Hurstpierpoint Village Band, marched solemnly to Stone Pound. All of the Druids, bar one, were attired in white robes and cowls the exception being clad in red. Several carried golden sickles, one a banner, and others bore the oak sapling on a stretcher.

The north-west corner of the crossroads had been provided for the purpose by Colonel W. H. Campion of Danny. The position had been prepared for the ceremony with a roped enclosure around the planting spot, beyond which was a platform, chairs for lady visitors, and a stand for bandsmen.

Speechmaking, prayers and hymns were the order of the day, followed by the planting of the little tree. When this was done, a commemorative tablet was placed at its foot, after which it was suggested that the spot might become immortalised in the manner of the nearby Friars Oak. It was even proposed that the locality's name be changed from Stone Pound to the 'Druid's Oak', or perhaps, 'Coronation Crossways'! and that members of the local lodge should create a tradition by re-visiting the site on an annual basis.

While the change of name never took place, the yearly visits did, at least up until the outbreak of the First World War, and from then on the young oak remained undisturbed until 1926, after which it was threatened by a proposed road widening scheme. The Druids came to its aid, and carefully lifting the sapling from the ground, conveyed it back to the village where it was replanted with due pomp and ceremony in the gardens of the Hassocks Hotel. During the proceedings, the provincial Grand Secretary of the Southdown Lodge, (Brother H. Searle) offered a sword to the Provincial Grand Arch Druid (Brother J. C. Clark) and charged him to take it and guard the tree against all adversaries. Refusing to accept the proffered weapon, Brother Clark replied:

> The Supreme Ruler of all will guard it.

It might have been better had he accepted the weapon, as now, many years later nothing remains to show that the sacred oak ever existed. And, like their tree, the Ancient Order of the Druids also appears to have vanished without trace, a curious circumstance when considering it was a national organisation that exerted undoubted influence on English social life in the earlier half of the 20th century.

The north west corner of Stone Pound crossroads – the site selected for the planting of the Druid's Oak

To the west of Stone Pound and on the north side of the road leading to Hurstpierpoint, there is a curious little mound that is so distinctly shaped as to look almost artificial. Named Buttinghill, it stands in the fields of Ham Farm, and has a history that can be traced back to Anglo-Saxon times when it was chosen as the site for an open air institution known as the 'Hundred' court. In those far off days, the 'Witan' was the supreme court in the land, next came the 'Shire Moot' and then the 'Hundred'. In the case of Buttinghill, the area in jurisdiction comprised Hurstpierpoint, Clayton and Keymer. Later it was extended to include Cuckfield, Crawley, Worth, Burlye Arches and Slaugham.

The system, which lasted many years, had its roots in the tenth century, when a monarch called Edgar, issued the 'Ordinance of the Hundred'. This had the effect of dividing the shires into smaller districts, and gave the inhabitants of each the authority to police the same, and to punish wrongdoers.

During the reign of William the Conqueror, the organisation known as 'Frankpledge' was evolved. This meant that every free-man had to be enrolled in a group of ten, and the members of these groups were collectively bound to produce those of their number who might be called upon to give evidence at the 'Hundred', or one of the senior courts. A so-called 'View of Frankpledge' was held twice yearly at Buttinghill and similar courts throughout the land to see that this was done.

The court officers consisted of local landowners who acted as judges, and included other important members of the community, such as the Reeve, who was elected by the villagers, and in addition to dealing with crime, these persons also served as a sort of local government, and could legally require work of a civic nature – such as road repairs – to be undertaken by named individuals or groups. Failure to comply was an offence punishable by fine, as may be gathered by the following extracts taken from the *Sussex Archaeological Collections*, which published surviving records of the Buttinghill 'Hundred' made in the year 1621.

1. That William Scrase has not thoroughly cleansed his ditch, nor has taken the water incumbering the King's highway into his great meadow below the church of Clayton, as he ought by the day at the last view given to him, so he forfeits 5 shillings.

2. That the farmers of the lands and tenements called Hammondes in Clayton are to repair a bridge near Hamons gate before the like day under penalty of 10 shillings.

3. That Henry Smith about the feast of St Bartholomew last past, by force and arms broke the pound at St John's Common in Kymer and took away divers animals, viz: one gelding and five wenyers impounded there by John Anstye, and he was fined 3 shillings 4 pence.

4. William Broderton and George Alfrey have deposited filth in the highway in the village of Cuckfield, and they are to remove it before the Feast of All Saints next, under penalty for each delinquent of 5 shillings.

These documents not only provide us with a fascinating peep into the past, but because of their date, also give an indication of the length of time the institutions remained in force.

Magnus Volk and John Saxby

Volks Electric Railway ~ School Superintendant ~ Pointlock system ~ Saxby & Farmer ~ Northcourt

Moving forward a few centuries and continuing with our journey, it will be noticed that a short distance on from the crossroads and to the right, a west-facing dwelling occupies the furthermost corner of Stanford Avenue and London Road. This property, a former farmhouse, was for a while the home of Magnus Volk, the famous inventor who moved to Hassocks with his family in 1903.

The eldest child of a clockmaker who hailed from the Duchy of Baden in the Black Forest, Magnus Volk was born in 1851 at his father's shop at 35 Western Road, Brighton. As he grew up he developed a boyhood interest in electricity that was to last for the rest of his life, an interest that one day linked both himself and his home town with the birth of the 'electric age'.

The most interesting point of his career commenced when at the age of thirty, he received public acclaim for a street fire alarm system. Then he became engineer to the Telephone Company and was responsible for introducing the telephone to Brighton. He also inaugurated private lines at Eastbourne, Bexhill and Hastings, with the result that the Brighton Corporation recognising his expertise, appointed him as the borough electrical engineer, in which capacity he masterminded the illumination of the Pavilion Buildings, by far the largest installation of electrical lighting in the country up to that time.

It was about then that he first became engaged in the project with which he has been associated ever since – the Volks Electric Railway (V. E. R.) and this it must be emphasised was at a time when electric traction was in its infancy. A number of experiments had already been made, but they had been unsatisfactory as the current available was only from primary batteries, and the electric motor was in a primitive state. However the eventual development of the dynamo and the third rail system for conveying electric power to trains made further progress possible. This was demonstrated most tellingly at the Berlin Trades Fair of 1879, when a small electric locomotive operating on a narrow gauge railway just nine hundred yards in length, successfully carried a total of eighty thousand passengers over a period of four months. Two years later a public line, one and a half miles long, and built by the same company (Werner Siemens) opened between Anhalt and Lichterfelde near Berlin.

Germany then was the pioneer nation with regards to electric traction, and Magnus Volk took advantage of both family and business connections that he had with that country when he laid his own line along the Brighton seafront in 1883. Running between the old Aquarium and the Chain Pier, a distance of approximately quarter of a mile, it was officially opened the same year and became the first public electric railway in Great Britain. Over thirty thousand passengers had used the service by the following January, at which time it was decided to extend the track beneath the Chain Pier, and to continue it for nearly another mile to Paston Place, where it terminated at the Banjo Groyne.

1893 saw the full flowering of Magnus Volk's imaginative genius. In that year he successfully promoted a bill in Parliament for a line to run three miles through the sea from the Banjo Groyne to Rottingdean.

The vehicle designed for this unique track more resembled a creation from the pen of Jules Verne than a railway coach, for the carriage used was 24 feet above rail level and mounted on four legs, two standing on each track, and each carried by four wheels. It was 50 feet long, 22 feet wide and weighed forty tons. One hundred and fifty passengers could be accommodated on a platform not unlike the deck of a moderate sized pleasure steamer. A trolley wire ran alongside the track and trolley arms conducted the electric current to four 25 horse power motors fitted on the deck. Life-belts were suspended from the wall of the saloon, and to complete the nautical picture, a life-boat swung on davits at the side.

The sight of the extraordinary looking craft perched on elongated

Daddy Longlegs

shafts, gliding through the waves, quickly earned it the name by which it has always been remembered – 'Daddy Longlegs'! Sadly the history of Volk's engineering marvel is all too brief. Only a week after the service had triumphantly opened, the great gale that struck Brighton on the night of December 4th, 1896, destroyed the Chain Pier, sweeping its wreckage round the Banjo Groyne to batter Daddy Longlegs at its mooring. Thousands of pounds worth of damage was caused and by the time repairs had been completed, all of the following year's summer trade was lost.

As if this was not enough, when it had finally been restored to working order, the railway failed to live up to the promoter's expectations. The reason being that technical progress was not yet equal to their grand conception, or put more simply, there was just not enough power available for the carriage to make rapid journeys at periods of high tide. From that point on it rarely went to Rottingdean, but was mostly used for taking passengers on short and rather slow rides over the sea.

When work started on improving and extending the groynes in 1901. It was discovered that it was not possible to raise the track sufficiently to cross them, and so the railway was abandoned. The car was broken up for its scrap value, the rails were removed, and only the concrete bases were left to mark the site. Now, with the construction of the Brighton Marina, these too have gone.

Much has been written about Magnus Volk, and nothing better than the biography by his son, Conrad. Within its pages one learns that in addition to being a brilliant inventor, and a keen man of business, Magnus was also the superintendent of the Hassocks Congregational Church Sunday School, the duties of which he fulfilled in a heartwarming manner. He was extremely fond of children, and they of him, as may be gathered from the following extract from Conrad's book:

> Among the many letters I have received while writing this record are some which recall those days, as the children saw them; very simply, maybe, but with a sincerity more telling than could be conveyed by any words of mine. I quote from a few of them.
>
> "'I must take this opportunity," says Mrs G. Markham, "of paying tribute to your father, a man whose kindness, and love of children, I shall always remember .... He lived quite close to my school, and sometimes invited my friends and me to play in his lovely garden. We certainly enjoyed ourselves. Treats for me in those days were rare, as my mother was a widow of forty-two, with a family of eight to bring up."
>
> Mrs Scott, who as May Thompsett, writes: "Spending my

childhood at Hassocks I saw him quite often ... All the children loved him, and he was surrounded by them wherever he went."

And from Mrs A. L. Purdie (née Charman): "It was a well kept secret. You can imagine our surprise and delight on Christmas Eve, when a knock came on the door, and my mother opened it to find a real live Father Christmas on the doorstep. He solemnly handed out four toys from his sack, one for each of us children, and then vanished into the night. We could hardly believe that it had happened. Nowadays children have so much and wouldn't take a lot of notice, but times were different then..."

They were indeed.

Magnus Volk

At this point of our journey a strange coincidence occurs. Just a little further along Stanford Avenue, a mere stone's throw from Magnus Volk's home, stood an imposing old property called Northcourt, and it was there from 1900, that another famous inventor – John Saxby – once resided until his death in 1913.

> You have done more than any man living in the reign of Queen Victoria to save human life.

This was the handsome tribute paid to him by the Prince of Wales (later Edward VII) at the official opening of the London Underground. Such fulsome praise was well deserved, for John Saxby was responsible for creating the pointlock, a safety apparatus that in conjunction with a signal box, prevents the points on a railway track from being changed while a train is passing over them. And it was at Keymer Junction that the first signal of the type was erected.

With regards to his invention – in an interview that was published in the *Mid Sussex Times* in 1909 – Mr Saxby had this to say:

> The idea of the interlocking system came to me after a mishap at Bricklayers Arms Junction, on the Brighton Line. By some means or other, which neither the driver nor the signalman could satisfactorily explain, a train was shunted onto the wrong line. The signalman gave the signal for the driver of the train to go on the Brighton line, and he proceeded to do so, but found the points had not been altered, and he was on another line. So he had to reverse his engine and return. It was a mishap that might have had disastrous results.
>
> For two and a half years after that event, I worked on my invention, which was such that the signals could not be altered until the points were altered.

Like his contemporary, Magnus Volk, John Saxby was born and bred in Brighton, and as a lad served an apprenticeship with a local carpenter. On completing his indentures, he went to work for the London Brighton and South Coast Railway Company, remaining in their employ for over twenty-five years, and during that time so,

John Saxby

impressed the management with his knowledge and practical ability that promotion quickly followed. His first important invention had to do with signal-making on the line, and he ultimately became the superintendent of that department.

Further inventions followed, including the interlock system which completely revolutionised the railway world, and caused his name to be bracketed with such well known men as Isambard Kingdom Brunel, Robert Stevenson, Sir John Fowler and Benjamin Baker.

Then – at the very pinnacle of a glittering career – he left the company to set up on his own in what had formerly been two timber sheds situated near the old Liverpool Hotel in Haywards Heath. There he set about manufacturing signals, signal boxes, and connections. Orders immediately poured in, and in such great numbers that it soon became obvious the premises were not large enough to deal with them. So without further ado, he moved to Kilburn where he built an immense factory and provided employment for two thousand men in the process.

At about this stage he entered into partnership with a Mr J. S. Farmer, and thus the firm Saxby and Farmer, a company that was to gain international repute, came into being and built a large factory at Brussels, and later another at Creil, near Paris. Contracts were won in places as far apart as India, Russia and Egypt. While in Europe, the Belgian government alone supplied them with an order worth £200,000 and when considering that in those days (1880) £1 sterling had a purchasing power approximately fifty times greater than £1 in 1998, the true value of the order becomes apparent.

It would also seem that the company can claim the credit for installing the first traffic lights in the country – in the middle of the road between Bridge Street and Great George Street, Westminster – for an article in the *Express* newspaper, dated December 8th, 1868, stated:

> Messrs Saxby and Farmer, the well-known railway signalling engineers, have erected a column 20 feet high, with a spacious gas lamp near the top, the design of which is the application of the semaphore signal to the public streets at points where the foot passengers have hitherto depended for their protection on the gesticulations of a policeman – often a very inadequate defence against accident. The lamp will usually present to view a green light, which will serve to foot passengers by way of caution, and at the same time remind drivers of vehicles to slacken their speed. The effect of substituting the red light for the green one, and of raising the arms of the semaphore – a simultaneous operation – will arrest the traffic on each side.

This however was not one of their most successful inventions, and failed to catch on. The place was chosen, it was said, for the preservation of the lives of the peers of the realm and MPs.

John Saxby retired to Northcourt in 1900 at the age of seventy nine,. He had lived to see his name become a household word in railway signalling and traffic working, so much so that for years to come, and long after his death, the signal departments of many foreign lines were known as Saxby departments.

Vigorous until almost the end, he died on the 22nd April 1913, and was buried in Wivelsfield churchyard alongside his wife Hannah who had predeceased him by thirty years.

Of Northcourt itself, nothing now remains, but in a further extract of unpublished autobiography, one of the authors of this book recalls his own childhood memories of the place:

> Built on the grand scale and approached from two directions by a bow-shaped drive, Northcourt was a fine example of mid-Victorian architecture. For several years it was the residence of the Rawlings family, a daughter of which was a gifted artist and a Royal Academician. Within its grounds stood a small lodge, the home of a Captain Garbett. He was related to the well known Archdeacon Garbett (of whom we will learn more later). The captain had a resident housekeeper by the name of Miss Cheal, and apparently this lady supplemented her income by running what can only be described as a small Dame School at the premises.
>
> In years to come, education was to play a more significant role at Northcourt, for after the Rawlings had departed and during the early stages of the Second World War, it was acquired by the De La Salle Order of Christian Brothers, which was a Catholic run group of private boarding schools for boys. One of their institutions was based at Southsea, and because of the German bombing campaign at nearby Portsmouth, it was decided to evacuate the pupils and staff to more peaceful climes – hence the move to Hassocks, where they became known as St. John's College, Northcourt.
>
> As well as the boarders they taught local boys, one of whom was my brother. The cost of his schooling was seven guineas a term, and the uniform consisted of a blue blazer, grey trousers and a cap that was quartered in alternate segments of dark and light blue. The Brothers wore black cassocks all of the time, both on and off duty, and these were decorated with what looked rather like two white bibs, one fixed on either side of the chest.
>
> For the information of parents, day boys received a weekly testimonial appertaining to their conduct and standard of work. Graded by colour, they were as follows: Pink: excellent, Blue: average, White: improvement is required!
>
> The teaching staff were well liked by the boys. There was however one exception, and he unfortunately was the headmaster. *Spare the rod and spoil the child* was his maxim in life and he adhered to it vigorously. His hobby was breeding rabbits, and the only expressions of tenderness he had ever been heard to utter were invariably addressed to them.
>
> But there were happy moments. As Christmas drew near, a yule log would be placed into one of the massive fireplaces and during the evenings, teachers and boys would sit round it for a rousing sing-song followed by cocoa and prayers. These last invariably included a blessing for King and Country and dear ones far away. We were all very patriotic then.
>
> At the end of the war, St John's returned to their former home at Southsea, and Northcourt was converted to a hotel. A large sign bearing its name used to stand at the junction of Stanford Avenue and London Road. Eventually however the rising price of land persuaded the owners to sell. As a result the building was demolished, a road laid through the grounds and the site of John Saxby's old home was covered in modern houses.

The Territorials

Summer Camp 1911 ~ P.V.B. Camp 1915

From this point of our journey, a line of cottages extends along the western side of the road almost as far as the Friars Oak. They were built in 1924 and on ground that once belonged to the Ham farm. Before that when field and hedgerow stretched uninterrupted all the way to Belmont Lane, it was a popular place to hold village fetes and sporting events. The Campion family of Danny who owned the land and the tenant farmer, Mr Horace Broad, were very community minded in this respect, particularly so with regards to the needs of the Territorials, battalions of which would march up from the coast to hold summer camps in these and other meadows in the district.

One might have supposed that the local people would have felt slightly concerned at the prospect of great numbers of soldiers arriving in their midst and indeed as we shall discover in due course – some did! But by and large, the men were well received, and the fact that their cheerful presence brought a touch of colour to the community is clearly revealed in a newspaper article of the period:

> If there is one thing about the Camp at Hassocks, of the 4th and 5th Battalions of the Royal Sussex Regiment, that has impressed the civilians more than another, it is the splendid behaviour of the 'Tommies'. When a great body of men – hundreds of them come out into the country for a fortnight's change from the ordinary rut and routine of life, certain allowances ought to be made for varying temperaments and boisterous spirits, but on all hands we have heard that the territorials who have been under canvas at Hassocks have done credit to themselves as individuals and to the Force to which they are attached. At Hassocks, at Hurst, at Keymer, as well as Ditchling, Burgess Hill and other places where residents have had the opportunity of noting the visits of the red-coated or khaki-clad citizen soldiers, the story told has been the same –"wonderfully well behaved, no disorder". Soldiers may perhaps be forgiven for chaffing a fine, buxom, nurse girl (and usually she doesn't mind it herself) and if on their way back to camp at night, arm in arm, they should burst forth into song, and declare that they 'won't come home til morning' – well, you just want to let them alone and they'll be all right! Yes, the Territorials are jolly good fellows.

Continuing in similar vein, the report describes some of the social activities that took place during the Battalion's visit. One such occasion was a garden party held for the officers at Danny Park, during which music was played by the Regimental Band. A sporting programme was also included, a feature being a novel tug-of-war contest between the local boy scouts and the soldiers – which the scouts won! It is only fair to mention that they outnumbered their opponents two to one.

Then the residents of the Mansion House at Hurstpierpoint, a Mr and Mrs Weekes, threw their grounds open, and tradesmen, farmers and others of the village, entertained the officers, the non-commissioned officers and the men alike. This seems to have been a particularly happy gathering, and in the words of the newspaper reporter, included, "a musical extravaganza supported by a number of most talented artistes". The report describes the venue as follows:

> In honour of the visitors, the grounds were delightfully illuminated, the paths leading to the central lawn being lined with fairy lights and with Chinese lanterns suspended from the trees. Around the lawns more fairy lights twinkled from amid the flower borders, while festoons of lanterns were arranged from the trees to a flagstaff in the centre. The southern end of the lawn, which is bounded by a battlemented wall, and a tower, a style of architecture which seemed so befitting to the occasion, were also prettily illuminated. As the evening advanced, these illuminations combined with the scarlet uniforms of the officers and men who were seated in groups, formed a most striking spectacle.

Sports Day held in the fields of Ham Farm, in about 1912/13. Belmont Wood may be seen in the background

The Territorials Summer Camp at Hassocks, July 1911

The last night of the camp is also nicely described:

> Many people visited the 'White City' during the last evening and some animated scenes were witnessed on the Hassocks Road. A pavement artist held a ragged cap beside his fine pictures, an action that was not in vain, for many Tommies cheerfully presented him with coppers. Scores of people were going in and out of the camp, where lights flickered and gave a softened glow from inside the bell-tents and huge marquees. Laughter and merriment abounded, while the distant sound of music and vocal refrain suggested that a concert was in progress. Indeed, the entire atmosphere resounded with good fellowship but as is always the case with jolly occasions, time sped swiftly by, and the moment soon arrived when the guests bade reluctant farewells. And so with 'lights out' our home defenders peacefully slept away their last night in the camp of 1911.

In 1915, just four years later and a momentous time in our country's history, the Sussex Home Protection Volunteer Brigade (The PVB) – a First World War version of the Home Guard – came to camp at Hassocks. After parading at Brighton Aquarium, the men, with greatcoats rolled and carried bandolier fashion over the right shoulder, marched, headed by a band and cyclist outriders, all the way to Ham Farm, where an advance party had pitched bell tents and marquees ready for occupation. But because of the war, their visit was mainly devoted to strenuous military exercises, so there was little time available for the sort of social activities that had been enjoyed by their peace-time predecessors. However, on the final full day, which was a Sunday, after attending a morning church parade, the troops invited the villagers to join them in an afternoon programme of sport to be held in the camp lines and the local people responded with enthusiasm. A response it must be said, that excited considerable hostile comment from some sections of the community, as became abundantly clear in the letter columns of the *Mid Sussex Times* , two examples from which are included here:

> (1) Sir – it is with sorrow that I heard from the lips of one of my Club girls, words to the effect – "O, miss, we didn't half have fun up at Hassocks on Sunday afternoon at the Home Defence Sports" – Even at this time of crisis the world is still forgetting God. Such deliberate Sabbath breaking is a serious hindrance to making our village a better and happier place, and I do plead against any repetition of such proceedings at either Hassocks, Hurstpierpoint or elsewhere.

> (2) Sir – A more disgraceful form of Sabbath desecration it is impossible to conceive. What do we find? Men, all over forty, and perhaps up to sixty years of age, participating in athletic sports on the Sabbath, and, as if to smother up the proceedings, uniting in the house of prayer immediately before doing so. On the face of it, it seems a mockery. One would have thought that men over forty would have done with athletic sports on any day, and would have had more serious thoughts of the nation's needs at the present time. I am afraid that the officers of the Hassocks camp could not have given a thought to the example they are setting to the younger generation.

In the meantime, and probably quite unaware of the furious outcry that their hospitality had unleashed, all those concerned had marched back to Brighton and dispersed.

Friars Oak

*The legend ~ The Tree ~ The Inn and some of its Landlords ~
The Farmhouse ~ Friars Oak House ~ Rodney Stone*

Like the Territorials we too must leave. Our next stop is at Friars Oak, a place where history has been supplanted by legend, because of the wrongful interpretation of the word 'friar'. The story often repeated and widely believed is that at unspecified dates in the past, friars from a local monastery would gather beneath a nearby oak and distribute alms to the poor. It is a charming tale, but it must be said that no evidence has yet been found to support the notion that either a monastery or religious order has ever existed in the area.

Messrs Mawer and Stenton are quite definite on the subject. A brief entry in their book on place names in Sussex, states that the vicinity was originally known as Frye's Oak, because of the association with the family of Agnes le Frye in 1327. A conclusion that Judith Glover in her book on Sussex place names agrees, adding only that the name le Frye means 'the freeborn'.

There is however no disputing that a huge and ancient oak once grew near the spot. With a girth exceeding fifteen feet it was a well known landmark and stood close to the entrance of the present golf course, where a footpath leads to Belmont.

The district, consisting of an inn, a farmhouse, a large private dwelling, a few cottages and little else, has, for such a small community, acquired an importance that is quite disproportionate to its size. An inn has stood on the site for about four hundred and fifty years. The present establishment was built over the cellars of the previous building, and at one time, was not only a tavern and a hostelry, but also served as a court of justice, and had a reputation of being the finest bull and bear-baiting house between London and Brighthelmstone. With reference to such matters, John Burgess, the Ditchling diarist, wrote in 1788:

London Road, 1954 – a time when cattle made a twice daily trip to and from fields near the Friars Oak to Hassocks Farm (now a garage and showrooms)

> Went to a bull bait at Fryers Oake, and there were plenty of wine and punch all the afternoon and a great many people.

It is said that the Prince of Wales (later to become George IVth) at the time of his residence at Brighton, frequently pulled up at the Friars Oak to watch the baiting, and that on one occasion, owing to heavy snowfall, was obliged to spend the night there. During those days – the golden age of the coach – the road resounded with the clatter of carriage wheels, and the inn with its diverse attractions, was a busy and prosperous staging post.

However, fortunes along the road were to change with the opening of the London to Brighton Railway. Businesses that catered for the coaching trade went into rapid decline. But not so the Friars Oak, the landlord there who was obviously a far-seeing man, set about converting his considerable acreage into pleasure gardens, some of the first to be opened in Mid Sussex, and the railway that had done so much to destroy his former livelihood, made amends by conveying train-loads of holidaymakers to Hassocks Gate, where they could enjoy a day in the country, and sample his hospitality in the process.

Not quite as ancient as the name suggests, this is the present pub, which was built over the cellars of the former posting house

Many respected landlords have held the licence at the Friars Oak during its long history. At the end of the 19th century, Mr Parker Marchant's was a well known name, then much later in the 1960s, Ron Cragg and his wife Joyce made the place a favourite meeting spot – a family tradition to be carried on by their son Malcolm in the 1990s. But before them, the host with the longest association with the pub was George William Jupp, a former builder and undertaker from Burgess Hill. Taking up the tenancy in 1903, he was to hold it for over thirty years, during which time, he and his wife made it a happy rendez-vous for customers far and near. Their genial hospitality combined with the excellence of the catering was such, that during the term of their tenancy, the pub became better known as Juppy's Place.

George Jupp was also a keen cricketer, and founded the Friars Oak Cricket Club. One of his sons, Valence William Crisp Jupp, received his early training there, and went on to become a brilliant all-rounder, gaining honours for Sussex, Northants and England. Valence Jupp was one of only two players (Freddie Brown was the other) to achieve the double of 1000 runs and 100 wickets in first class cricket for two counties: for Sussex (1920-21) and Northamptonshire (eight times between 1925 and 1933).

Another son, Mervyn, also a fine sportsman, distinguished himself by gaining the DCM in the First World War, and later gave his life for his country.

Clayton Parish had always attracted George Jupp, he loved its leafy byways, its shady paths and its fields beneath the rolling downs. Therefore it came as little surprise to his friends, when upon retiring in 1934, he stayed within shouting distance of his old home by moving over the road to nearby 'Bretforton' (named after his wife's native village in Worcestershire) where remained until his death in 1942.

Directly opposite the pub, a tree-lined drive leads to Friars Oak Farmhouse, a fine old building that was erected in 1805 (the year of the Battle of Trafalgar). No evidence has been found to suggest that a dwelling stood on the site before that date, although early records show that a sixty-acre farm called 'Fryers Oake' certainly was in existence as far back as 1624, for in that year it was noted that a lady called Frances, the wife of Richard Luxford, inherited the place by the will of her father, Thomas Brewer of Horsham.

In the 1990s, virtually all of the farm fields on the western side of the road were converted into a golf course, the development of which uncovered much of archaeological interest, including a hitherto unknown section of Roman road. In addition it has been suggested that at some time, the area could well have been an important fishing base, an assumption that if correct, raises considerable speculation as to how the landscape would have looked in those far off days, a subject on which the experts may ponder for years to come. In the meantime, what can be said with certainty, is that before the authorities caused the roads to be tarred, the brook that rises at Clayton and flows past the Friars Oak on its journey to the Adur, was considered to be one of the finest trout streams in the county.

Friars Oak Farmhouse, 1953

Friars Oak Farmhouse – which for nearly thirty years was home to one of the authors of this book

Adjoining the London Road a little to the north of the Farm and on the same side, there is a property thought to be early 19th century in construction. It was originally called Friars Oak Villa, was later changed to Friars Oak House, and in *Clayton – A Short Manorial History* , an unpublished work by the late Hugh Matthews, it states that the land upon which it stands was once a copyholding known as Plump John's. Regretfully though, no further information exists concerning this intriguing name.

For a period between the two World Wars, Friars Oak House became a guest house or hotel called 'The Flying Elephant', and at about that time, one of the occupiers , a rather odd young man, loved to dress up as a cowboy and gallop round the district on his horse, firing blanks from six-shooters' at startled passers-by. Cyril Charman recalled that he particularly liked to discharge his pistols while riding through Archway Tunnel at the foot of Woodlands Road, presumably because of the dramatic acoustic effects. It was a state of affairs that could not be allowed to continue, for although meaning no harm, this noisy 'Tom Mix' of Hassocks was regarded by many as a confounded nuisance, and it would seem that their remonstrations reached the appropriate quarters, for to the bitter disappointment of the local boys, the roar of colt 45s ceased as suddenly as they had begun, and peace returned to the village.

It should be recorded that the novel *Rodney Stone*, by Sir Arthur Conan Doyle was set at Friars Oak and along the Brighton Road. This historical adventure spans the last years of the 18th and the early years of the 19th centuries. Rodney Stone relates the story, but the real hero is Boy Jim Harrison, the apparent nephew of Champion Harrison, the blacksmith and ex-pugilist, and it is with Jim's fortunes that the book largely deals. There is a good plot and some thrilling scenes, two boxing contests in particular are wonderfully described, as is the race along the London Road between the coaches of Sir Charles Tregellis and Sir John Lade. In short it is an excellent yarn, but not one that should be regarded as a safe source of information for those interested in local history.

Friars Oak House

***Right**: New Close Farm Cottages between Hassocks and Burgess Hill. The carter was Frank Sayers of Hurstpierpoint*

New Close

Farmhouse ~ Hotel ~ Ice skating carnivals

The trout stream referred to earlier flows past the rear of the Friars Oak pub, and then twists and turns to the north before curving back in a westerly direction towards the road. In the process of its meandering, it passes through the grounds of New Close, a dwelling that was originally built as a farmhouse in the 17th century. This property, formerly a portion of the estate that belonged to Squire Cripps of Novington, was sold after that gentleman's death, and in the 1880s was sold again to Mr W. Claude Johnson, an entrepreneur who turned the place into a hotel. He built a considerable extension, one of the features being a billiards room. In addition, he installed an electrically powered clock at the northern end of the house, a time-piece that according to a newspaper report of the period:

> can be distinctly seen from the London to Brighton main road, and which is a great boon to the general public.

Further extracts from the report read as follows:

> A little to the south of the house, a very picturesque lake has been formed for boating etc. and during the long frost of the winter 1890, a great many persons from Brighton and other places enjoyed skating on it. Last winter a small sum was charged for its use, and the amount accruing is to be expended on enlarging and improving the lake for that purpose. When finished it will be about five acres in extent.

Ice skating on the frozen ponds and lakes in the district was a popular winter pastime in those days, and Mid Sussex contained many places that were suitable for the sport, namely at Cuckfield Park, Lindfield, Slaugham, St George's Retreat, Ditchling, Danny and Pondlye, and several more besides. But until the advent of Victoria Lake at Burgess Hill, the best of them all was the extensive sheet of water at New Close, which during the skating season averaged over five hundred visitors a day. So great was the interest

New Close Hotel

that in 1893, a series of late-night ice skating carnivals were held in aid of the Sussex County Hospital and other worthwhile causes. That these functions were immensely successful may be gathered by the following extract from an article that appeared in the *Mid Sussex Times* in January of that year.

> The officers and men of the Burgess Hill and Mid Sussex Volunteer Fire Brigade were present in uniform (representing one of the institutes in need of help) and undertook the duties of the gate and attended to the fires and lights. The Burgess Hill Brass Band were again in attendance, snugly ensconced in a wagon, and played right merrily as long as they could. Quite a little army visited the ice during the afternoon, but the carnival proper commenced soon after dark. It was then that the fancy dresses began to appear, and they were much more numerous and varied than at Thursday's carnival. The ice covered about five acres of water and a part of it being in serpentine form, made it a roomy and pleasant resort for

the skaters. As the evening advanced the numbers largely increased, and at nine o'clock the masquerade was in full swing. It was a sight well worth a visit, even if one could not skate, being so novel and so weird. Lights of all types were burning and Chinese lanterns were carried by many of the skaters. The company has been adequately described as follows:

The best and most commanding figure was perhaps, Mr Johnson himself (the proprietor) who, as a gay Charles II Cavalier, heartily entered into the proceedings, carrying an electric-lighted fairy lamp, and at times a Chinese lantern. The athletic figure of a Pierrot would glide after a suspicious -looking Sergeant of Police. Grey-headed Uncle Ned, the negro, and a cowboy would perhaps chase after a bewitching Mother Shipton and nearly come to grief over a spritely little clown, one of the best dresses of the night. Red Riding Hood and the Queen of Diamonds would chat with a diminutive White-Eyed Kaffir, prettily dressed young England skaters glided along like Dutchmen and maidens of the Zuyder Zee. The cocked hat of a Field Marshall would be in company with a highwayman, while military officers both native and otherwise, were as plentiful as the greatest military enthusiast could desire. Father Christmas, with a few cowled monks, a Pink Domino, and the ermine and scarlet cloak of an earl, would flutter besides a mantle suggestive of a patchwork counterpane. Huntsmen were also in evidence, and a beautiful lady in dainty white wool, possibly the Snow Queen, with attendant suite, would piquantly beg for pins, as she was 'coming all to pieces'. There were many costumes too fanciful to describe, some of the skating cloaks of the ladies being exceedingly pretty, both in colour and design.

It was indeed a gay and jolly time, and an evening that will live long in the memory of all who took part.

New Close continued to operate as a hotel until just before the outbreak of the First World War, then in 1916 it was purchased by James Robert Pace and reverted once more to farming use. The new owner would seem to have been a compassionate man, for he had additional stables purposefully built to provide holiday accommodation for London working horses. Four generations of his family were to live at New Close, with the result that the premises became so identified with them, that rather as in the case of George Jupp at the Friars Oak, the farm was referred to by one and all as Pace's Place.

Hammonds Mill and Clayton Priory

Business Venture ~ Fable ~ General Patton-Bethune ~ Public Debt and the Local Board ~ Fitz-Harry

Mr Johnson, the man responsible for converting and extending New Close, also had a controlling interest in Hammonds Mill on the other side of the road. There had been a water mill on this site for many years, in fact it probably preceded New Close, for it is mentioned in the Buttinghill records of 1615, when the miller, John Haselgrove, was called upon by the court to repair Eylesford bridge (which our road crosses).

Mr Johnson's involvement with the mill was that of a person intent upon improving and updating the business. He invested in modern equipment, extended the range of products, and changed the name – all of which was backed up by an extensive advertising campaign.

Hammonds Water Mill shortly before it was demolished

The *Mid Sussex Times* for several months carried an advertisement with a beautifully illustrated heading that read:

> New Close Steam Mills (lately known as Hammonds Mill)
> I beg to inform gentlemen farmers, corn dealers, bakers etc. that I am prepared to supply flour, offals, and all descriptions of corn, cake, hay, straw, chaff and also ground barley, ground oats and meal at the lowest possible prices. For quotations and particulars apply to me at the mills. J.R. Dodson, Manager

How successful the venture was is unknown, but it is unlikely that it operated for all that long, and certainly by the time that Mr Pace arrived on the scene, the mill had reverted once more to its former name, and any connection with New Close would appear to have been severed.

On the crest of the hill to the north of New Close is an entrance to a drive, a rather grand entrance, with a pillar on either side, each mounted by a sculptured eagle. From beneath their frowning gaze, a pleasant tree lined avenue runs past the gatekeeper's lodge in a westerly direction to Clayton Priory. This handsome dwelling, once a favourite meeting spot for the Southdown foxhounds, should one might suppose, have an interesting history. But apart from the unusual circumstances of its construction – more of which will be said later – it has none, or at least, none that the authors have been able to discover. However, there are always the fables! It has often been suggested for instance that long ago the place really was a priory or religious house of some sort – even that it was associated with the Friars Oak. But like the story of the good-hearted monks who reputedly distributed alms at that address, the tale is entirely without foundation. The facts of the matter are that the premises were built, and the grounds landscaped, as a mansion house for the Hammonds estate at the conclusion of the Napoleonic Wars in 1816 or thereabouts. No property of any description stood on that site before that date.

Whether by coincidence or not, many of the occupants of Clayton Priory have been military men, one of whom, General Walter D. P.

Clayton Priory

Patton-Bethune could have stepped straight from the pages of a *Boys Own* magazine. Rising swiftly through the ranks, he became Colonel of the 74th Regiment of the Highland Light Infantry and in the Crimean War, served on Lord Raglan's staff – but not as a 'deskbound warrior'. Twice he narrowly escaped death when his horses were shot from beneath him, and the gallantry he displayed on those occasions was mentioned in dispatches. His Crimean medal bore clasps for Sebastopol, Inkerman, Balaclava and the Alma. He also took part in the capture of the Peiho Forts in China and then went on to command a brigade during the Indian Mutiny. This was followed by promotion to Brigadier and a posting to Burma. Upon being made General, he became the youngest such officer in the army.

At the time of his retirement, the growing town of Burgess Hill was experiencing teething troubles, and many strongly worded complaints were being addressed to the Cuckfield Board of Guardians, the authority in those days that was responsible for governing the sanitary state of the area, particularly with regards to health hazards arising from cesspools, bad drains and pollution of local ponds and streams.

Little was done until after the passing of the Public Health Act in 1879, when it was agreed that a local Board should be formed to tackle the problems. That the members of this new Board went to work with gusto, is demonstrated by the fact that they immediately borrowed sums of money amounting to £15,000 to buy land and construct a sewage plant at Bridge Farm and Freaks Farm, and then laid five miles of sewers to serve the same. More money was borrowed to build a Board room and offices, together with accommodation for the surveyor in Church Road. Then a further £200 was spent on the acquisition of sixty lamp-posts to illuminate the area. Not content with that, they also proposed to construct five and a half miles of pavements at an estimated cost of £5,000, which would also be borrowed.

All of this was too much for the General. He was one of the old school of outspoken officers and was particularly antagonistic to the formation of a Local Board for Burgess Hill. He would have shot the lot of them if he could, for their proposals meant a considerable increase in the rates, and his land extended a great distance along the road. As it was he discarded sword for pen and engaged in a campaign of letter-writing:

> 'This scheme is totally unnecessary, he wrote in a communication to the *Mid-Sussex Times*, and is only adding a debt to the monstrous sum of £24,000 that has already been expended (on sewage plant and offices). The greatest curse that ever fell upon Burgess Hill has been the creation of this Local Board, owing to which, and the heavy rates caused thereby, many householders have been caused to fly; the consequence being a heavy fall in the value of house property, which will take many years to right itself. The nauseous odours in the vicinity of St John's National School are worse than ever; the smoke arising from the brickyards without chimneys is an unquestionable nuisance; and the flames of fire are most dangerous. If the £5,000 proposed to be spent on the footpaths were applied in buying up these brickyards in the vicinity of the main roads, it would confer an unquestionable benefit on the district, and then, and then only, would Burgess Hill become a flourishing place and a popular sanatorium, and then would be the time to discuss the footpaths.

The General was not the only person to express strong feelings, but he was one of the few who had the courage to identify himself. We say this because in those days it was an accepted custom for letters to the Editor to be published under pseudonyms, such as 'Nemo', 'One who Knows' 'Chatty', 'Uno 'Tis So', and many more in similar vein. One of these, a correspondent who described himself as Fitz-Harry, wrote a series of long and scurrilous letters, which appearing in the *Mid Sussex Times*, referred amongst other things, to the activities of the Local Board, the condition of the roads, and the pall of smoke that hung over the town. The following short extracts give an idea of his style:

> (1) They describe Burgess Hill as a very pleasant place. Well, so it is – the mud is only a foot deep, and the air is

deliciously perfumed with smoke from the potteries – that smoke which gets into your eyes and nose and down your throat. Oh! It makes my mouth water to think of it."

(2) I know everybody, hear everything, see what Burgess Hill is becoming. I could tell you tales and legends connected with this town. I could meet some tradesmen in the street and tell them what they do. I could tell the unwary traveller at what shop he won't and at what shop he will get cheated. Perhaps some time I may unfold the records of the place, known only to a few; but now I've written enough for the Burgess Hillian to consider and consider well as to what kind of place he lives in, and what part he plays.

As can be imagined, such florid prose produced an outraged response, and the columns of the *Mid Sussex Times* were inundated with repudiations and angry demands to know who precisely this Fitz-Harry was. It was even suggested that he was a fictional creation of the editor – drummed up to increase the readership of a still young newspaper, a suggestion, it must be said, that was vehemently denied.

Perhaps then it came as little surprise, when on the following November the fifth, in addition to Guy Fawkes and amidst a chorus of boos and jeers, a huge and unflattering effigy bearing the label Fitz-Harry was paraded round the town, and later consigned to the flames.

The Reverend J. P. Bacon-Phillips

Prince of Letter Writers ~ The Tramps' Parson

A familiar figure to be seen walking our road, (and indeed, many other roads in Mid Sussex) between the two World Wars, was a former clergyman by the name of J. P. Bacon-Phillips. He was by all accounts, a tall athletic looking man, who upon retiring from the cloth, had moved to Burgess Hill, having spent the previous twenty-eight years of his life as the rector of Crowhurst. Possessed of a robust physique, a keen intellect and a kind and compassionate nature, he was known and admired in stratas of society that had little or nothing in common, for included amongst his numerous friends and acquaintances were people as socially diverse as the great editors of Fleet Street and the most humble and illiterate of tramps. The former welcomed his contributions to their publications while the latter were grateful for his generous and unstinting charity.

The Tramps' Parson,
the Reverend J. P. Bacon-Phillips

Dubbed the 'Prince of Newspaper Letter-Writers', the signature and address, J, P. Bacon Phillips, Burgess Hill, Sussex, was known to readers of 'Letters to the Editor' in the daily and weekly press throughout the country and his name beneath a submission invariably meant that it was worthy of attention.

His hobby started in 1889, when he had an anonymous contribution printed in the *Mid Sussex Times*. Forty-five years later, his published letters had run into tens of thousands, covering nearly everything under the sun and because he was considered to be an authority on a multitude of matters, his name was frequently quoted in periodicals and magazines both at home and abroad. A communication to the *Daily Telegraph* that referred to 'Curfew bells' [1] prompted seventy-seven published replies, which at the time represented the greatest response to any letter that had ever appeared in a British newspaper.

A reader of the old *News Chronicle*, rather peevishly enquired of the editor, as to the number and type of subjects on which the reverend gentleman was qualified to express such "expert" opinion. The answer he received was brief and to the point:

> Many – and varied.

Bacon-Phillips was a character in an age of characters, and the essence of the man is revealed in an interview that was reproduced in *Mid Sussex Through the Ages* by A. H. Gregory. Talking of life generally and letter-writing in particular, the learned cleric stated:

> I took to it regularly in 1892, dealing with the subject of witnesses being bullied by counsel in the courts. The Witnesses' Protection Society and General Legal Reform Union sprang out of that correspondence. Once I saved a Swiss workman from the gallows. The man had been sentenced to death for dropping his baby over a London bridge, but through the agitation I started with my pen, the sentence was commuted to one of penal servitude for life – and he was afterwards freed. I have strongly defended little children, tramps, the aged poor, cabmen, busmen and animals, particularly horses. I advocated that children under a certain age should not be allowed in public houses, and my suggestion that the children's clause in the Licensing Bill of 1908 should be embodied in a separate Bill resulted in the Children's Act. It had been thrown out by our legislators. I have probably interviewed more centenarians than any man in England, to find out their modes of living, and I came to the conclusion that their chief points were – walking regularly in the open air and moderation in eating and drinking. I walk ten miles a day. I am old-fashioned. To me walking is a pleasure and a mental and physical stimulus. It is Apostolic. I do not like to see a clergyman flying about on a bicycle. Some years ago I was discussing the relative merits of motor-cars and horses with the conductor of a motor-bus. '"You could not imagine," he said. "Queen Victoria driving in a motor-car. It would not have been dignified – but there Sir, dignity died with Queen Victoria." You could not imagine either, any of the apostles riding bicycles or any of the monkey-on-a-stick devices of the present day. My correspondence has led me to receive many abusive letters and threats of violence – one threatened to shoot me and another to give me a horse-whipping – but some have been highly amusing. Once when I wrote of the 'honoured office of domestic servants and the becoming nature of a cap and apron,' some of the 'honoured' ones sent me caps and aprons and told me to practise what I preached!

Bacon-Phillips always claimed that the countryside of Sussex was his favourite subject, and as we have already learned, he walked ten miles of it every day. His sensibilities therefore were somewhat offended, when in 1922, it was suggested in the press that the clergy were flabby and effeminate. "I could produce 100 clerical representatives of the Church of England," he said, "who for physical fitness, mental alertness, breadth of view and knowledge of human nature would rival any of the other learned professions – army, navy, law or physic." He then challenged anyone who felt inclined, to a ten mile walking contest, saying that he would donate £10 to charity if beaten. To the surprise and delight of many, the Succentor of Southwark Cathedral, the Reverend T.P. Stephens, picked up the gauntlet and it was provisionally agreed that the event should take place on the Brighton Road. However, when the date was finally announced, the bold Mr Stephens had second thoughts, and withdrew from the lists.

We mentioned earlier that the reverend gentleman counted tramps amongst his friends. He in turn was their friend, and not only that, but their chaplain and champion also. In addition to being the knowledgeable and witty 'Prince of Letter-Writers,' Bacon–Phillips was equally well known as the 'Tramp's Parson'. He met hundreds of them on the road many of whom were making their way from the Brighton Workhouse (or Union as it was called) to the similar establishment at Cuckfield, or the other way about. State payments to the needy had not then been introduced, so it was his opinion that these unfortunate wayfarers should receive assistance from the church, but as this quite obviously was not forthcoming, he endeavoured to help them himself. When meeting these gentlemen of the road he would talk to them, offering friendly words of encouragement backed up with small gifts of pipes and tobacco. He also gave them tickets – which he later redeemed – that could be used to obtain food and tea (but not alcohol) from shops along the way.

> Many of these men, he said, are eighty years of age; they walk from ten to twenty miles a day; and most of them are in wonderful health. It is almost as rare to see a dead tramp as a dead donkey!

Thus spoke the Reverend J. P. Bacon-Phillips, and upon reaching the age of eighty himself, he lived just one more year before passing on in 1938. His funeral was held at Crowhurst, and six men of that village, dressed in Sussex smocks, met the coffin on its arrival from Burgess Hill. They then transferred it to a farm wagon and in the traditional manner of which he would have surely approved, their old parson made his last journey back to the church.

[1] The Curfew Bell was, in the olden days, rung in towns at 8pm in the winter, and at sunset in the summer, to give warning that all fires should be put out, and all lights extinguished as a precaution against fire. It was a practice that was introduced into England by William the First (The Conqueror) and in some places the traditional sounding of the bell was continued into the 20th century.

Hammonds Place

Ancient manor ~ Piracy and plunder

Carrying on, we enter the crowded suburbs (once field and park-land) that herald the approach to Burgess Hill, and here, surrounded by new dwellings, stands an ancient and picturesque house which it is said, in Elizabethan days was named 'A-woods' or possibly, 'Atwoods' but is now known as Hammonds Place. This partly timbered property with its Horsham stone roof is undoubtedly one of the oldest buildings in the district, and probably one of the oldest we will pass on our journey. The porch entrance which can be seen from the road, is Elizabethan, and on the stone jamb of the doorway – almost obliterated by age – are the initials, E.M. They surely denote Edward Michelborne, the person who is credited with building the premises, although it is possible that he just extended an even older dwelling that stood on the site. Above the porch is a carved shield which bears the arms of the Farnefold's – the family from whom it is thought his mother-in-law was descended – and high on the gable is inscribed the date: 1566.

The shape of the house has changed over the years. In Edward Michelborne's time it was considerably larger, but in the 19th century its southern side was demolished in order to provide building materials for the construction of Clayton Priory. A picture by S. H. Grimm depicting this southern side prior to its pulling down, has been reproduced in Edward Buckton Lamb's *Studies of Ancient Domestic Architecture* .

With regards to the age and structure of the property,Viscountess Wolseley, in an article she wrote for the *Sussex County Magazine*, sought the opinion of of Mr Walter H. Godfrey, F.R.I.B.A.

> and he - with his usual kindness - tells me this picture of 'Grimm's' showing the long wing that existed to the left of the porch and also a return wing parallel with the timber one on the north side, made the building originally a quadrangle. He says: "From this I am inclined to think that the 1566 work included a reconstruction of an older timber

> wing, which was dismantled and re-roofed. All the work in Grimm's view is stone and brick and Elizabethan in character.

The right honourable lady went on to say:

> This coincides with local hearsay repeated to me by Mrs Whittle, who spent some years of her childhood at Hammonds Place: for she had heard that the house consisted of two wings and a chapel, and that a courtyard with a fountain in it was once in the middle between the two wings.

However, to return to Edward Michelborne. His son, Sir Edward Michelborne, would appear to have been a particularly bloodthirsty ruffian. In the *Dictionary of National Biography*, edited by Simon Lee, he is described as an adventurer who, having obtained the Kings licence to trade with the countries of the far east, set sail in 1604 in command of his ship, the *Tiger,* and then, betraying the trust that had been placed in his authority, enriched himself by plundering and piracy on the high seas. This included a savage attack on a Chinese junk in which several of his crew, and all of the Chinese, perished. It was his nefarious activities that probably gave rise to the legend that within either the house or gardens of Hammonds Place, treasure of some description lies concealed.

Hammond's Place (from a drawing by Grimm)

Not destined to enjoy his ill-gotten gains for long, Sir Edward died in 1609, and bequeathed many handsome gifts to both children and servants alike. One beneficiary, a Mr George Pryse, received the intriguing legacy of, "20 angells[1] and my cloke lined with black velvet." But perhaps aware that his had been a mispent life, this errant knight ends his will on a somewhat bitter note, when he says that he takes his leave of, "this miserable world".

[1] The angells that Sir Edward bequeathed to George Pryse, were not heavenly messengers but old English gold coins.

The Board School

Archdeacon Garbett ~ Mary Hare

Travelling on we enter Burgess Hill, a town that has vastly changed from the smoky 19th century 'mud-bath' previously described by Fitz-Harry and others – and a town that continues to change. For example, south of the junction with Station Road, on a spot that is now a residential area, there once stood an imposing old school. It was a building of ecclesiastical appearance, deliberately so, for when erected by subscription in 1850 as a board school it was intended to serve a dual purpose, in the week, as a seat of learning for poor children to be educated in accordance with the principles of the Church of England, and on Sundays, as a place of worship. A schoolmaster's house was attached, also accommodation for the clergymen at weekends. How well the arrangement worked is not described, but it could hardly have been easy, and there was probably a collective sigh of relief when the new church of St. John the Evangelist was finally consecrated thirteen years later in 1863.

With the Education Act of 1870, and the formation of the Clayton and Keymer School Board for the united parishes in 1873 an infants department was added to the building. That is more or less how it remained until the early 1950s and the development of Oakmeeds Community College, before which the senior section of the old London Road School, not only catered for the children of Burgess Hill, but also for the youngsters of Hassocks, Clayton, Keymer and even Ditchling.The entire number of these out-of-town pupils was transported to and fro daily in a bus, so ancient and unreliable, that its passengers were regularly required to disembark outside of New Close, then if the old vehicle managed to make its way up the hill, they would climb back on board for the final leg of the journey.

Prior to 1850 and the construction of the afore-mentioned school, educational facilities for working class children in the area were extremely limited. The first 'Free School' to open on weekdays in the district was believed to be that created by the Venerable James Garbett, the Archdeacon of Chichester and the Rector of Clayton and Keymer. Largely due to his efforts, a range of old stables – a remnant of the coaching era – that stood nearly opposite the junction of Station Road, was converted into a school cum church, where, according to A. H. Gregory's *The Story of Burgess Hill*, the Archdeacon "preached with power and success". Known locally as the Stable-church, the establishment also had a choir, the musical accompaniment to which (again according to Gregory) was the clarinet of Mr Charlie Stone (of the ironworks) and an instrument described as the 'grandfather fiddle', played by a Mr White.

When the children and the church services were transferred to the new Board school, the old building was used first as a shop and then later as a warehouse before it was finally demolished in 1895. A terrace of cottages was erected on the site by Mr Edwin Street, a local butcher and farmer and reputedly the largest man in Mid Sussex, a person who was to later become more widely known as the proprietor of the Victoria Gardens[1], a pleasure resort that in its hey-day was easily the most popular holiday venue in the county.

Education remains the theme as we penetrate further into town. Having passed the entrance to Victoria Road - which was also built by Edwin Street with the intention (unrealised) of extending it to Hurstpierpoint – we come to the junction of Victoria Way, a comparatively new road that leads into the industrial estate. A modern concrete structure that serves as a bank, stands on the corner now, but once it was the site of a substantial Victorian dwelling called Dene Hollow, a building that in its day was regarded as one of the finest properties in Burgess Hill.

[1] A subject that has been comprehensively dealt with in our book – *Edwin Street and the Victoria Pleasure Gardens,* also published by Mid-Sussex Books

The old Board School at Burgess Hill

It was here in 1916, that a lady by the name of Miss Mary Hare, opened a private co-educational school for deaf and dumb children which had residential accommodation for approximately forty boarders. The spacious grounds contained playing fields, an outdoor swimming pool, orchards and vegetable gardens, while the curriculum in addition to the standard subjects, included carpentry, domestic science, dancing, the various field sports and swimming. Miss Hare was assisted by specially qualified teachers, and her staff included medical and dental officers as well as resident nurses and specialists. The school was successful from the outset, so much so, that it was soon attracting pupils from overseas, a fact alluded to by A. H. Gregory in *The Story of Burgess Hill.*

> Miss Hare at Dene Hollow, has a splendid school for deaf and dumb children coming from all parts of the world – her methods and achievements being simply marvellous.

Mr Gregory did not exaggerate. The fact is testified in an amusing extract from a letter written by Mrs Eileen Bennett, née Woods, who was employed there as a nurse-maid in the 1930s. According to her, one of the pupils at the time, a girl by the name of Swrendra (whose nickname was Birdie) was the daughter of a Maharajah from the Punjab, and Mrs Bennett went on to say:

> There was a funny story. In 1935, the Maharajah was in London for the Silver Jubilee of King George V and Queen Mary, and sometime after we were told that Birdie's father was sending mangoes to the school. Now in those days mangoes weren't known about much in England, and we hadn't any idea what they were, however, Mrs Browne, the housekeeper, told us nurses to put on clean uniforms on such a day as the 'Mangoes' were calling on the school to see us all! You should have seen her face when the car pulled up and the chauffeur brought in some boxes bearing the word "MANGO" – we had a good laugh over that.

The reputation of the school continued to grow, and in 1946, the year following the founder's death, it relinquished its private status and under the Education Act of 1944, became the first Grammar School for the Deaf in Britain. Three years later in 1949, its leavers

Dene Hollow

were preparing for the school certificate examination, something that no group of deaf children had ever attempted before. The occasion was covered by the *News Chronicle*, and a representative from that paper visited the school to file a report on their progress. That report, extracts from which are included here, serves as a worthy tribute to Mary Hare, for without her vision, energy and perseverence, it would never have been written:

> Yesterday I watched the twelve girls and boys of the sixth form, ten of whom are stone deaf, 'listening' to their science-master's lecture on the splitting of light, and not missing a word. He fired questions at them and they answered him. It was uncanny. The secret is a combination of lip-reading and speech practice. But for this new training they would have gone through life using the deaf and dumb sign language and making strange noises or no sound at all. Pupils range from 12 to 18 years and

In 1949, Deryk Taylor, leader of the 1st Ditchling Troop, invited scouts from the Mary Hare School to camp with his lads at the County Rally which was held at Telham park. The Mary Hare boys are to the left of the picture. Deryk Taylor stands second in from the right

come from every part of the country. All have found their voices and speak like ordinary children. At daily assembly they say prayers and sing hymns in tune. They even dance the waltz, valeta and polka to music they have never heard. Last Christmas they went carol singing like other children. They mix with school-children in the town. Masters and Mistresses are all especially trained in oral teaching. The curriculum includes English literature and composition, French, history, geography, religious knowledge, civics, general science, mathematics, Latin and art. There are a dozen clubs, from mothercraft to bee-keeping – nobody going among them would guess their handicap.

Mary Hare

The Pottery Town

A place of desolation ~ A place of industry ~ Pug mill

Burgess Hill according to Charles G. Harper in his book, *The Brighton Road:*

> sprang up, if not quite with the rapidity of a Californian mining town, at least with a celerity almost unknown in England.

He was clearly unimpressed with the locality, as a few pungent remarks reveal. The inhabitants for instance are described as "land - grabbing mushroom townsfolk", and the area we know as Fairfield Recreation Ground, "a place of desolation covered with ant-hills and a receptacle for the potsherds[1] of the community." He concluded with the observation:

> We shook the dust off this rising brick-making, tile and drainpipe manufacturing place from off our feet and made haste to leave it behind.

Harper was unfair, but to make allowances for his ill-humour, the neighbourhood must have come as rather a shock. After all, one moment he was being transported through the rural beauty of Mid-Sussex and commenting on delightful villages and hamlets that had hardly changed since Shakespeare's day and the next, he was bumping along the road in a region of clamorous noise, choking smoke and incessant labour – a sort of southern version of the "dark and satanic mills!"

The reason for this industry was twofold; a natural resource of good quality clay, and the coming of the railway. These crucial factors transformed what had been a rural backwater into a hive of commerce and activity. The town became saturated with brickyards, clay-pits and potteries, they were everywhere – on both sides of Station Road (a thoroughfare that was originally called Potters Lane), in the vicinity of St. Wilfrid's Road, along London Road, and to the east of the district, near Keymer Junction. This last, as described by Gregory in *The Story of Burgess Hill,* was quite an extensive operation:

> Engine houses, kilns, lofty shafts, drying sheds and various other buildings were erected and railway lines laid to connect with the branch railway, whilst about three hundred workmen, four engines and a dozen brickmaking and other machines were employed. There was every conceivable development in the art and mystery of pottery manufacture, designs that could not be effected by hand being wrought by machinery of the most elaborate description. Nor was the comfort and well-being of the employees overlooked, for in the precincts of the yard were erected many cottages, and a schoolhouse for the instruction of the children.

With regards to the western half of the town, a glance at an ordnance survey map showing Burgess Hill as it was in 1873/74, gives a clear indication of the industry's dominance of the area. For example, it can be seen that virtually all of the land between the junctions of Station Road and Church Road, extending eastwards to what is now Civic Way, was being utilised for pottery purposes. Another large tract of land on the opposite side of London Road was being worked in a similar fashion, and it is there, tucked discreetly from view behind the Royal George Public House, that a little 'pug-mill' the only surviving building of the era, stands to this very day. 'Pug' for those who are unacquainted with the expression, was the name given to clay being mixed to make bricks.

The mill, a hexagonally shaped premises with a conical roof, has a distinctive appearance, which suggests that the power for the machinery, would have been provided by a captive donkey or mule made to walk endlessly round the perimeter wall. There was a time when the task of 'mixing' was conducted in a much simpler manner, according to Gregory:

> Many of the early clay-workers at Burgess Hill came from the North and the West, and it is reported that they shocked the natives by their primitive ways of living. One particularly bad custom was stopped by Archdeacon Garbett – that in which young boys, with their bare feet, trod out the clay before it was shaped.

[1] The potsherds were fragments, or shards, of broken pots, i.e. (pot and shard).

After ceasing to be used in the manufacture of pug the mill has served many purposes, most notably that of headquarters for the Burgess Hill Scout Troop, in which capacity it was used until well after the Second World War. That it still stands says much for the determination of those who wish to preserve the unique heritage of the district.

Burgess Hill, the pottery town

Burgess Hill Scouts moving into their new HQ. The pug mill is on the extreme right

The King's Head

The first Post Office ~ St. John's Sheep and Lamb Fair ~ Chapel Cottage

On the northern border of Burgess Hill, we pass the oldest inn in the district, a former posting house called The King's Head, a place says Gregory, that:

> ...if it could speak, could tell many a story of old Host Pagden's eccentricities and his adventures with the rogues and vagabonds that infested the district in his time. Host Pagden hanged himself in his stable. Host Hubbard, Host Stepney (of the good old white round frock order of publicans), Host Pronger (who left the country for his country's good!) and Host Budd were among the publicans of The King's Head scores of years ago. Host Budd particularly wished to be buried in his own garden, and he was eventually laid to rest in the burial ground of St. John's Chapel, only just over the hedgerow of his garden at the time.

The first Post Office in Burgess Hill was contained in the first shop, and that, still used as such, stands opposite to the Inn. However, at the time of which we write, the area had hardly developed at all, and letters to the neighbourhood were invariably addressed to 'Burgess Hill – near Hurstpierpoint', and were delivered from that village by a postman with a small mail cart drawn by two dogs. There were no letter boxes in those days, so he would announce his arrival by blowing on a post-horn, and anyone wishing to send a letter would bring it out to him, pay the necessary postage, and that was that.

Continuing northwards the road descends Fairplace Hill. On land nearby, an event took place that caused the name of St. John's to be known long before the turnpikes, railways, potteries or anything else that has so far been mentioned. We refer to the 'St. John's Sheep Lamb and Cattle Fair', a fixture held annually on the 5th of July since time immemorial. Strictly speaking it was a 'cull-lamb fair' as the flockmasters brought only their smallest lambs, saving the bigger and better animals for the much larger fair that was held a

The old Post Office

month later at Lindfield. This had always been the practice and doubtless would have continued but for the construction of that great arbitor of change, the railway, which, because it made Burgess Hill so much easier to reach, caused buyers to arrive in droves and to become as thick on the ground as the sheep they sought. Indeed, the demand was such that the supply had to be considerably increased, and in due course St. John's became one of the principal lamb-marts in the county, drawing livestock from places as far apart as Findon in the west, and Hastings and St. Leonards to the east. Pleasure Fairs, says Gregory, were also in attendance, and judging by his description, would seem to have been merry if somewhat noisy occasions:

> When the Southdown Shepherds came to Burgess Hill, clad in their smock frocks, carrying their Pyecombe-made crooks and their large faded umbrellas, and attended by their sagacious looking sheep dogs, they had the time of their lives before returning to their bucolic haunts; they could even compete with the natives in quaffing pints of beer – and that was saying something in those times! – and they would sing 'The Farmer's Boy' and other old

Heading north out of Burgess Hill

songs which echoed over the countryside from the vicinities of the public-houses.

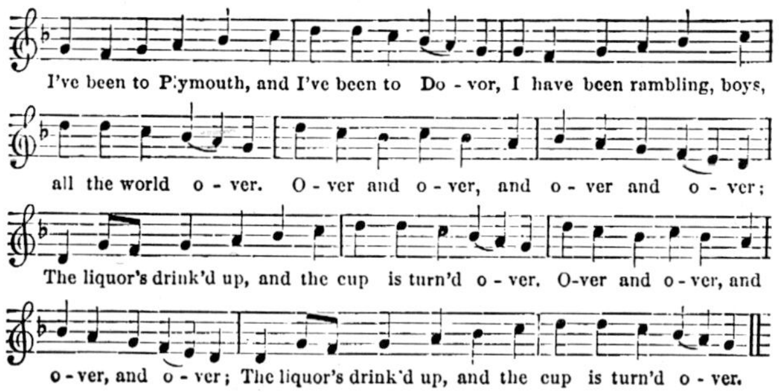

Meanwhile the air was also charged with the brazen-throated 'music' of roundabout organs, the coarse and challenging shouts of exponents of the 'noble art' at boxing booths, the raucous shouts of showmen, and the cracking of rifles and the smashing of bottles at the shooting galleries.

Not surprisingly perhaps, there were those who were less than enthusiastic regarding such carryings-on, as may be gathered by the following protest bearing 135 signatures which was delivered to the offices of the Urban District Council in 1895:

> Gentlemen: We, the undersigned ratepayers, visitors and inhabitants of St. John's Common, Burgess Hill. Beg to call your attention to the nuisances existing at the Fair Field through the letting of the same to the travelling shows, the gipsy fraternity and others. The discordant noises proceeding therefrom having a tendency to drive people away from the locality. The sanitary arrangements are simply disgraceful, no respect being paid to private property or feelings. Trusting you will use every legal means to abolish the nuisance is our earnest wish.

A person who surely had first hand experience of the events described was George James Roderick White, a resident of Chapel Cottages down Fairplace Hill. He earned his niche in Mid Sussex history by proclaiming that on the day the First World War ended, he would climb onto the gable of his house and stand on his head – which he did! Mr White, a rather eccentric character, loved to speak in quotes and one he repeated to the point of tedium, was:

> George James Roderick White - always right, never tight!

An expression, bearing in mind his roof-top activities, that was best taken with a pinch of salt!

George James Roderick White

Abbotsford Tea Gardens

Webbs Park ~ The Royal Mail Parcel Coach ~ The Beast of Pilbeam Wood

A little to the north of Chapel Cottages, the highway forks. To the right, Isaacs Lane leads to Haywards Heath, skirting the former site of St. John's turnpike gate in the process, while our road bears to the left and almost immediately passes Abbotsford School, a premises that nowadays is hardly accorded a glance. How different to the 1930s! Then it was a regularly attended tea gardens, containing not only extensive grounds through which visitors might stroll and admire beautifully tended flower-borders, rock-gardens and lily-ponds, but also enjoy the attendant attractions of an aviary and a monkey-house.

Bordering Abbotsford is Hook Place, an establishment that since 1949 has been the head office of the International Bible Training Institute, a society that had its origins in Leamington Spa.

The property was formerly known as Webbs Park, and back in the 1890s it was by far the most popular holiday venue for miles around, continuing to do good business, even after the opening of the infinitely superior Victoria Gardens in 1897. Mr R. Rogers was the proprietor, and the fact that he gave the public what they wanted is borne out by newspaper reports of the time:

> (1) Webbs Park was thronged yesterday by about 1000 children and friends from Clarendon Villas Mission Hall, Hove, who headed by the recently formed Christian-workers Brass Band, marched to the Park from Burgess Hill Station where they arrived by a 'special' train.
>
> (2) Yesterday the children of Church Road Baptist Chapel had an outing to Webbs Park. With their teachers and friends they were conveyed thither in wagonettes, spending a most enjoyable afternoon. The 'Olympian Circle' and other amusements provided by Host Rogers being much patronised."

Looking south from the junction of Isaacs Lane with Cuckfield Road

The Olympian Circle never really caught on, despite being described as one of the greatest novelties of the kind in vogue, and it has proved difficult to obtain any clear details about the apparatus. However, to the best of our understanding, it consisted of three circular and quite separate metalled tracks laid parallel with each other, one used for boating cars. another for saddleback cars, and the last for swimming cars. As they were not connected, there was no interference with the different methods of locomotion. Apparently the riders supplied their own motive power and the cars were so arranged that races could take place between any two of them.

Mr Rogers must have been an innovative man, for another, probably unique amusement to be found at Webbs Park was a riding machine described as a 'Mustang Pony'. Again, apart from its delightful name, it has been impossible to discover much about it. The little we do know is that it was both invented and manufactured at a business premises in Burgess Hill called the "London Road Ironworks" and that before it was installed at the pleasure-gardens, local children were invited to spend an evening at the workshop to have a test ride!

In an article published in the old *Tinsley's* magazine, Mr W. Wilson-Tickle, who rode on the box seat of the Royal Mail Parcel Coach which nightly traversed the fifty-two odd miles between London and Brighton, described the moon-lit views of the Sussex countryside as the "gem of the journey," especially those seen from the road linking Clayton and Cuckfield. "It was," he said:

> ..as choice a piece of real English scenery as can be found; hedgerows, grand trees, undulating country, with here and there a glimpse of the lordly homes of England.

His enthusiasm might not have been so fulsome had he been passing through the vicinity during the period of the "midnight howling!" For there was a time – in 1911 or thereabouts – when local people were being aroused from their slumbers by a recurrent and unearthly screaming apparently emanating from Pilbeam Wood. The noise was so horrid, that according to a farmer's wife:

> it made my blood run cold.

Lyes Farm

The cause of the sound was obviously animal, but precisely what sort was not easy to say. Armed with shotguns, some men from the district including Mr Upton of Lyes Farm and his son, Syd, entered the wood in the small hours, determined to resolve the matter once and for all. They were not kept waiting long. Having taken up their respective positions, stealthy movements were heard where the undergrowth was at its thickest. Then without any warning, a large shadowy shape dashed by where young Syd was standing.

The startled youth raised his rifle, but too late, for with incredible ease, the beast said to be quite five feet in length and with a bushy tail, leaped over a five-bar gate and disappeared across a field. A few nights later, ghostly howling was heard at Wineham, and later still in Pickwell wood. After which it ended as suddenly as it had begun, and the creature, whatever it might have been, disappeared without trace.

As can be imagined, there was considerable conjecture regarding its identity, until that is, a soldier home on leave from India, having heard the tale, ventured the opinion that it could have been a jackal! He might have been right, for it later transpired that just a few years earlier, because of a dearth of foxes, cubs had been introduced locally from abroad, and a young jackal – if such it was – could well have been one of them.

Farmer George Upton of Lyes Farm in a family portrait. Syd Upton is sitting on his father's knee

Moon Hill

Harvest Hill ~ Riddons Farm ~ Mount Noddy

From here-on, the road winds through countryside that despite the alien presence of monstrous electricity pylons, is surely as lovely now as when described by Mr Wilson-Tickle during his night-time journey. Nestling in this idyllic spot and set a good distance back from the thoroughfare is a fine old dwelling known as Moon Hill. This establishment was at one time the residence of Mr Walter Lloyd, a gentleman who is credited with inaugurating the Haywards Heath Horse Shows of the past, and in so doing, making the name of the town famous in equine circles. It was also the former home of a family called Lampson, and Mrs Lampson became widely known as a musician with the women's institute movement during its early years.

Overlooking Moon Hill, and most of the surrounding area, is another superbly situated premises called Harvest Hill. This elegant property "is a 'beau ideal' meeting place for hounds" according to a report of a stag-hunting meet in the 1890s, which then went on to say:

> The view from the hill is a magnificent one. On Saturday the atmosphere was clear, and the Weald lay beautifully distinct. The South Downs, of course, filled in the landscape in the distance. To the left the view lay over the Haywards Heath and Wivelsfield district, beautifully wooded. In front the sight wandered over St. John's, and the housetops of Burgess Hill shewed in clusters through the trees several miles away. To the right front lay Hurst College and the village of Hurst beyond that, a fine hunting district. On the immediate right lay the Sussex Lake, Pondlye, and a prospect of miles of beautiful country. The hundreds of spectators were charmed with the view on the fine spring day, and many discovered, for the first time, that Harvest Hill was a beauty spot of Sussex.

The resident, Mr Thomas William Best, or Tom Best as his friends called him, was the owner of the Talbot Hotel and the Dolphin Brewery that formerly stood in Ockenden Lane, Cuckfield. Before relinquishing that business and retiring to Harvest Hill, he had lived in the town for many years, where in addition to his commercial interests, he was a church warden, Chairman of the Cuckfield Local Board and Chairman of the Gas Company. In fact he was quite an institution in the district, being regarded more like an uncrowned king. And it was a monarch's munificence that he lavished upon the guests who attended the meet to which we alluded.

Harvest Hill

It was the last run of the season and a visit by the Surrey Staghounds. A train known as the 'Stag Special' brought the visitors to Haywards Heath and from there they made their way by road via Cuckfield to Ansty, and the white house of Harvest Hill, which

Moon Hill

according to the report:

> was virtually besieged. The roads were lined with carriages and vehicles. Horsemen and pedestrians flocked in from every side. The stabling and farm-buildings were filled, the house meadows were filled, and even the grounds and flower gardens were filled. The huntsmen and hounds trooped in upon the lawn, and the hunting picture was complete. Not only outside, but inside, Harvest Hill was thronged. Neighbouring gentry, landowners and farmers, clergymen, squires and knights of the shire, lawyers, County Councillors present and future, rubbed shoulders with the heroes of the pigskin[1], and shared the hospitality of Mr Best. The white-haired Squire of Harvest Hill is hospitality itself, and never was a hunting breakfast enjoyed as was the breakfast on Saturday. For was it not the last run of the season, and was not the master, jovial Tom Nickalls, king of the largest meet he had ever called together – excepting one perhaps. And after such a welcome the hunters had received, no wonder the toast given by the master – "Here's the health of Mr Best" – was received so lustily. And when Mr William Wood, in glowing eloquence, gave "The health of the Master," no wonder the very foundation of Harvest Hill shook with the cheers of the huntsmen.

A mere step from Harvest Hill the road slopes past Riddons Farm, a place that for several years was home to one of the authors of this book, and a holiday home for the other. This fine old building, unpretentious, yet beautiful in its simplicity, could have been that described by E. B. W. Chappelow in a poem dedicated to an unnamed cottage near Cuckfield:

> A house adze hewn and moulded by man's hand,
> A lovely relic in a lovely land.

Childhood memories of vacations spent at Riddons during the 1940s recall a world and way of life that has well-nigh vanished. It was a time when during the evenings, family and friends would gather round the table in the spacious parlour to discuss the doings of the day, and perhaps play a hand of Newmarket or Nap, games that were invariably enlivened by humorous small-talk and friendly gossip. A sense of timelessness prevailed over those occasions, a feeling that it had always been thus and always would, a state of mind brought on no doubt by the murmuring voices with their distinctive Sussex dialect, the measured ticking of the clock, and the soft lamplight reflecting on the iron fireback, a handsome old relic with the date 1622 and the initials S. W. C. engraved thereon.

Upstairs there was a favourite hidey-hole known as the 'secret room', so named because the paper on the wall was also pasted on the back of the door, thereby making it almost impossible to detect. Outside in the yard, the bull, a mighty creature with a curly brow, watched impassively from his pen as cows with swinging udders plodded past on their way to be milked. Chickens fussed and scratched in the straw, farm cats darted silently amongst the outbuildings, and from a row of hutches at the side of the house, a musky, slightly rancid smell, betrayed the presence of ferrets, cold hearted little killers every one, with sinuous snake-like bodies and eyes like shiny pink beads.

The road passing Riddons Farm – Ted and Henry Upton displaying their horses

[1] A 'pigskin' is a saddle. To throw a leg across a pigskin is to mount a horse.

The farm bailiff, Mr Syd Upton – he who had been involved in the hunting of the supposed jackal – was a countryman born and bred. Originally trained as a gamekeeper, he possessed an impressive knowledge of his domain, and probably knew the location of every birds nest and rabbit hole on his land. His son, Boy, "a chip off the old block", inherited all of his father's skills, and more besides. It was always a treat to accompany him on a pigeon shoot, cartridges were rarely wasted, and to watch his spaniels retrieve the fallen birds and then lay them at his feet, so gently that hardly a feather was ruffled, was to marvel at the rapport between man and dog.

Fishing was another pleasurable pastime, despite the odd location of the pond. This, rather curiously was situated in a crater-like depression, that must have made it difficult for cattle to reach, and an angler glancing up at the circle of sky above could have easily imagined that he was standing in an extinct volcano! The catch was usually restricted to tiddlers (small gleaming roach hardly large enough to provide a cat with a supper) but monsters lurked far below. In the twilight of a warm summer's evening, huge carp, wily old fish with thick protuberant lips that had never been scarred by a hook, would rise from the depths to gorge on insects which basked on the surface. The peculiar slurping noises they made when gulping down their prey sounded like pebbles being dropped into the water.

Mount Noddy, Ansty

Our next port of call is not very far away, the place being a small cottage with the quaint and ancient name of Mount Noddy. Standing in an elevated position at the side of the road just north of the hair-pin junction with the lane to Hurstpierpoint, the property faces due west, as apparently do many others throughout the country that bear the same or a similar title. According to historians this is because a deity called Nod or Nud was the Celtic sun god or god of the setting sun, and at one time all sites that bore his name were considered to be hallowed ground and had sacred edifices of some sort erected upon them.

Ansty

The Old House ~ The Green Cross Inn ~ Ansty Farm ~ Miss Louisa Best ~ Ansty Lullaby

The road now ascends to Ansty, a small hamlet that is situated in the southern half of the rural parish of Cuckfield. The name Ansty, or Ansty on the Hill as it was once called, is very old and there have been various suggestions as to its origin. It is still not known with certainty which is correct, but the authors tend to support the view that it is derived from *An* a Saxon name, and *tighe*. which is old Saxon for paddock or enclosure. Hence we may infer that *An's tighe* was a farm or enclosed land belonging to An and it all developed from that?

Perhaps one of the first properties to catch the traveller's eye is a picturesque timber built house that, half concealed by shrubbery, stands on the island in the centre of two roads and opposite the garage. Called the "Old House" it gives a pleasing welcome to the area. By raising one's head, it will be seen that high up on the wall is an inset stone, on which is carved the legend, 'N.I.M.1727' (with the N. over the I.M.) This suggests that the place may well have been built by the Nordens, a wealthy family who were once Lords of the Manor at Marshalls in Cuckfield. And although mere speculation on our part, it is tempting to identify the property as being the home of the actress at Anstye Cross in Conan Doyle's *Rodney Stone*, a dwelling, said to be a good four mile walk from the Friars Oak, that was described as:

> The cosy little house: all honeysuckle and creepers, with the wooden porch and the lattice windows.

The inn that stands at the village centre is comparatively speaking, new, the original establishment described by local historian the late Hubert Bates, as:

> The old 'Green Cross' Inn, with its flagstone tap-room, its great oak settle, and the still older tales that were told round the huge open hearth, has, alas gone.

The name, Green Cross, at least was retained for many years, but now that too has changed – albeit only slightly – to the Ansty Cross. This name is rather odd considering the original sign alluded not to the location, but to the badge of the Hussey's, a notable family who served Sussex as members of Parliament, and held other public offices for the best part of 300 years.

The Old House, Ansty

The building that Hubert Bates describes as the most important and interesting house in the district, is Ansty Farm. Of this he says:

> It has a long history reaching back into the misty past; in fact it may well have been the original *Ans tighe* and it appears in some of the oldest surveys of the manor simply as 'Anstie'. Details in the building show that it is of two periods, and, fortunately, the two dates are to be found. Down in the cellar, under the older part, is a large carved stone bearing the initials G.T.E.1713: (with the G over T.E.). This may signify that it was built by Thomas Gates, who held the freehold for several years before that date. High up on the gable of the north wing is another stone with the date 1768 carved in relief, and the work there

The original Green Cross Inn, Ansty

Ansty Farm, the oldest property in the district

This grim visaged pair were Mr and Mrs Young, former 'mine hosts' of the old Green Cross Inn

> suggests a later period. This north wing has one of the most handsome gables and carved barge boards in the neighbourhood, and with its long row of dentils is really a beautiful piece of work. The whole of the house is splendidly built with squared stonework to the first floor and weather tiling above, except in the north wing, where the oak beams are exposed down to the stone plinth at ground level. There is no doubt that, when built, it was a house of considerable pretensions.

Despite being in the shadow of Cuckfield, Ansty has always guarded its separate identity, and in this it has been aided by numerous benefactors whose generosity and community spirit over the years, have made the spot the pleasant place it is. Sir Harry Preston, the Brighton hotelier who resided at Appletree Cottage was one. Major H. H. Blaker of Ansty Place was another, and there were many more. However, no history of the little hamlet would be complete without reference to Miss Louisa Best, who, during her long life took a keen and active interest in the welfare of the local people, and threw herself wholeheartedly into any scheme or project that would help improve their lot.

Her most lasting contribution is the church of St. John's, which, was erected at her expense and dedicated in 1909 by the Bishop of Lewes as a tribute to her father, Tom Best of Harvest Hill, a gentleman with whom we have already been acquainted.

Her influence was felt everywhere, and not least in the organisation of the popular concerts that regularly took place in the mission room. These were well produced functions that unfailingly played to packed houses, with many of the patrons walking all the way from Cuckfield to enjoy the entertainment.

After her parents' death, Miss Best moved to Well Field, a property she had built near the centre of the village, and a residence that, because of her passion for chess, was to become a mecca for exponents of the game throughout Mid Sussex. She and her brother, Tom Best Jnr., died within two days of each other, and with their passing, the family's link with the parish, a happy association that had lasted for more than 150 years was finally broken.

Miss Louisa Best

The Mission Church, Ansty

The former Mission Room

ANSTY + MISSION + ROOM.

THURSDAY, APRIL 23RD, 1896,

AT 7.30 O'CLOCK.

PROGRAMME.

PART I.

PIANO DUET	"Sleigh Race"		
	MRS. MORGAN AND MISS LOUEY BROOKS.		
SONG	"My Darling was so fair"	Taubert	
	MISS KEATING.		
SONG	"Old Timber-toes"	Cecil Tovey	
	REV. W. G. IRVINE.		
SONG	"The Swallows"	Cowen	
	MISS LOUEY BROOKS.		
READING	"Love in a Balloon"		
	REV. E. R. D. LITLE.		
SONG	"Tell me my Heart"	Bishop	
	MRS. MORGAN.		
VIOLIN SOLO	"La Serenata"	Tosti	
	MR. MOWBRAY.		
SONG	"Butterflies"	F. Corbet	
	MISS KEATING.		

PART II.

SONG	"An Andalusian Maid"	Philp
	MISS LOUEY BROOKS.	
SONG	"The Three Sailor Boys"	Theo Marzials
	REV. W. G. IRVINE.	
SONG	"Carmencita"	G. Lane
	MRS. MORGAN.	
READING	"A Sleeping Beauty"	
	REV. E. R. D. LITLE.	
SONG	"Dere's only one Moon in de Sky"	Lovett King
	MISS KEATING.	
VIOLIN SOLO	"A Stray Thought"	H. Farmer
	MR. MOWBRAY.	
SONG	"Wishes and Fishes"	Roeckel
	MISS LOUEY BROOKS.	
SONG	"The Owl"	Stephen Adams
	REV. W. G. IRVINE.	
SONG	"When Love is kind"	A. L.
	MRS. MORGAN.	

A concert programme, organised by Miss Louisa Best

Hubert Bates shall have the last word on Ansty. That he loved the place is clearly revealed by his affectionate and informative articles. Nowhere is this better illustrated than when he chanced to hear a woodcutter's young wife singing a lullaby to her baby child. Touched by the words, he set them down and this is what he heard:

The sun has set o'er Chancton Hill
And sleepy is the daffodil
Hushaby, hushaby-by

In Pucksroade now the fairies sing
And dance around a silver ring.
Hushaby, hushaby-by.

The moon pops up behind Moon Hill;
His face is laughing, laughing still.
Hushaby, hushaby-by

He's getting up, as we shall see,
To look't himself in great Pond Leigh.
Hushaby, hushaby-by.

Its dark as night in Pickwell Wood,
Sleep my little one, sleep is good.
Hushaby, hushaby-by.

While mother asks dear God on high
To keep the babes in Old Ansty.
Hushaby, hushaby-by.

Leaving Ansty on the road to Cuckfield

High Bridge

High Bridge Mill ~ Major Floyd and the Home Guard

The road now runs downhill, and at its lowest point bridges a stream. Back in 1970 this was a notorious sight-seeing spot, for in that year the crossing, known as High Bridge, collapsed, and in so doing cut Cuckfield off from the south, When the authorities calculated that to rebuild it would take several months, an anguished howl of protest arose from the town traders. In an attempt to ease the situation, an army R.E.M.E unit spanned the gap with a Bailey Bridge. This allowed a trickle of traffic to get through, but did little to help the complainants, who continued to air their grievances until such time as the road was properly re-opened.

The stream originally provided the power to turn the wheel at High Bridge Water Mill, an establishment that lies a short distance to the east of the road. The first owner of this mill, Mr Jacob Caffyn, commenced operations back in 1811 when he used the premises for grinding corn. Later it was to be demoted to grind coarser grain and cattle meal, and continued in this humbler capacity until 1930, at which time it closed for business.

Major Floyd

A private residence ever since, the mill-house has had several owners, one of whom, an ex-army officer known as Major Floyd

The Ansty Home Guard, 1943, photographed outside the Village Hall

had the reputation of being rather eccentric. Many stories have been told about him, and the one repeated here concerns his relationship with the Home Guard during the Second World War. Evidently believing that its members were insufficiently alert while performing their night-time duties, and therefore needing pepping-up, he took it upon himself to lay concealed amongst the hedgerows from where he would spring up like a Jack-in-the-Box and lecture passing soldiers on the importance of constant vigilance.

That his intentions were honourable is obvious, just as it is obvious that those unlucky enough to be on the receiving end would soon weary of the man's Blimpish[1] behaviour. Ex-Major or not, it was felt that something had to be done. So one dark night, as the old warrior, crouched low to the ground, was making his way stealthily through the shadows, he was suddenly pounced upon by a Home Guard patrol, and marched to their headquarters where he was placed under close arrest. He discovered too late, that the men of Sussex were not to be trifled with – as indeed did one of their officers, who having become rather overbearing in his manner, was debagged[2] in Pink's Wood!

1 The term *Blimpish* derives from Colonel Blimp, a fictional army officer representing a pompous elderly figure, a type of diehard or reactionary.

2 To debag is to remove the trousers of a person as a punishment or a joke.

Cuckfield

The Swimming Club ~ The Sussex Iron Industry ~ Cuckfield Park ~ The Workhouse ~ The King's Head ~ Ockenden Manor and Timothy Burrell ~ Coaching Days

To the east of Highbridge Mill, in a shadowy depression of ground that has run wild with nettles, scrub and other rank growth, a footbridge crosses the stream, and a rambler pausing at the spot would never guess he was standing near the site of the former Cuckfield Swimming Club, an institution that was closed for health reasons during the 1950s. Down at the water's edge, evidence of its former existence can still be seen, such as the foundations of the dam that once raised the level of the brook as it flowed into the pool, while emerging from the brambles on the bank above and looking rather like a Ma'yan ruin, is a small concrete structure that probably housed the purification plant.

It is thought that in the days of the Sussex iron industry, the area was flooded to serve as a hammer-pond for a nearby forge. Then, in 1906 or thereabouts, it was acquired by a group of publicly minded persons whose intention was to convert the place into a bathing station for the use of the local people. Known as the Cuckfield Improvement Association, this group either renewed or repaired the existing dams, lined the pool with concrete, erected a spring board, and installed a purification plant. The venture was successful from the outset. A caretaker was employed, changing rooms were built, and except for the duration of the two World Wars, galas were held there annually. It is still remembered with affection by senior citizens of the district, one of whom, Miss Rose Powell, recalls:

> Before the Burgess Hill Lido opened in 1935, there were no swimming facilities in the area, except for Stroods and the Birch Hotel, both of which were expensive and difficult to reach by public transport, hence the popularity of Cuckfield's swimming pool. This was reached by a footpath that skirted the sewage farm, a place that we invariably hurried past with noses thrust deep into our towels, and although the pool was in close proximity, thankfully it was protected from unpleasant odours by a steep bank and intervening foliage. On gala days the water's edge would be lined with cheering spectators, while on quieter occasions we would share it with the resident water-voles, delightful little creatures that swam close to the bank and interfered with no-one Not so delightful, were the horrid horse-flies, that hovering overhead would swoop down on unsuspecting sun-bathers.

To look at the lovely meadows and woods surrounding Cuckfield now, considerable effort is required to realise that once it must have been a truly hellish region denuded of trees and covered by a constant pall of smoke. Yet this was assuredly the case, for in the days when the Black Country of the Midlands and the North were unknown, Sussex and parts of the adjoining counties were the seat of England's iron industry, and the smelting furnaces were fed not with coal, but charcoal from the southern forests. By day the woods echoed to the lumberer's axe, the quarryman's pick and the din of hammers; by night the sky was red with the glare of fires. Around Cuckfield, the sites of such places – generally situated on the bank of a stream – were numerous, and can easily be recognised by name, such as Furnace Wood, and Bellowsnose Wood and Cinder Bank.

The ore, hewn from the rock, was wheeled to a furnace to be thrown into a brick-built kiln where for several hours it was burned with charcoal to purify it. The next step was to the blast furnace, a great square tower, which, built against the hillside, was filled with charcoal and limestone, and kept burning at a high temperature by constant blasts from huge bellows operated by water-wheels. Because heating these furnaces to the correct degree took several weeks, they were kept constantly burning, year in and year out. The iron stone was put in at the top and as the iron melted, it sank to the bottom, and at intervals the liquid metal was poured into channels of sand where it was allowed to cool. As it cooled, and while it remained soft enough to work, the metal would be cut into smaller or larger pieces called 'sows' and 'pigs'; hence the term 'pig-iron'.

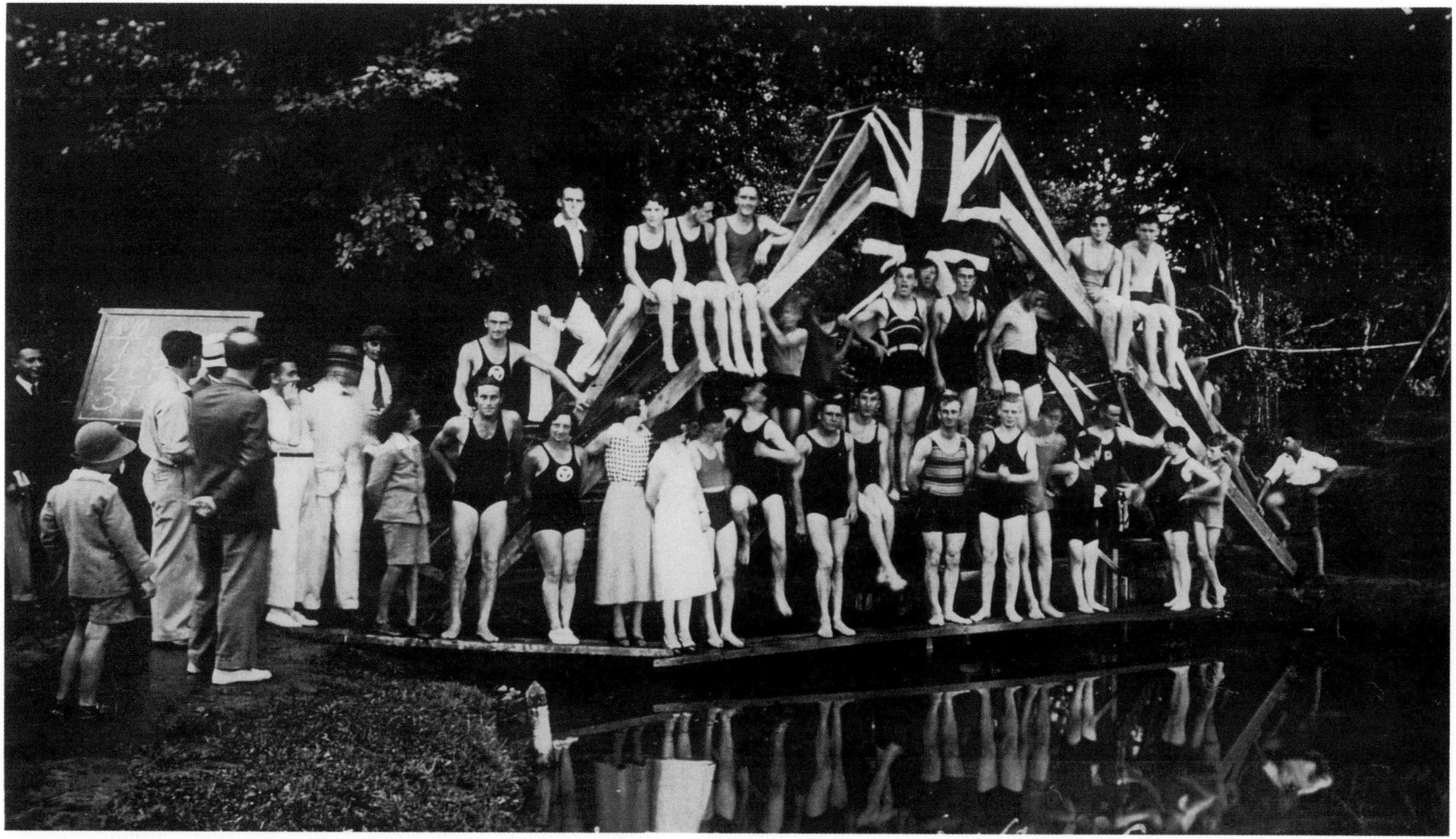

Cuckfield Swimming Club, annual gala, 1933

The industrial barons of the day – known as Ironmasters – made their fortunes out of the process, and none more so than Henry Bowyer who built Cuckfield Place (now Cuckfield Park) back in the 16th century. Since his time much has been written about the mansion and its various occupants, especially the Sergison family, therefore we will restrict ourselves to one story only, a strange and barely credible tale that nevertheless is absolutely true. The source of the information comes from an article that was published in the old *Sussex Express and County Herald*:

> Many houses have their ghosts, and the novelist, Harrison Ainsworth used Cuckfield Park in his novel *Rookwood* which featured atree with supernatural powers. But how many houses can claim a "suppositious" child? Who else amongst the wealthy and respected families of Sussex have narrowly escaped having a poor little unwanted heiress palmed upon them? This is what happened in Cuckfield early in the 19th century, the drama ending with the exposure of the innocent child in the High Courts before no less than the Lord Chief Justice.
>
> It began when Colonel Francis Sergison, the younger brother of the wealthy owner of Cuckfield Park, having dissipated the great part of his fortune, went to live in Dublin. Thrown into jail for debt, he met there the beautiful widow of a coach-builder who had suffered a similar misfortune. She told him her troubles and he comforted her. They fell in love and were married within the walls of the prison, but were in time released and lived according to the court report "in circumstances of pecuniary difficulty."
>
> This did not prevent the colonel however from yearning for a daughter or a son, or the resourceful wife from satisfying his wishes. Helped by a servant, whose tongue she later silenced by an annuity, Mrs Sergison purchased a newly born baby girl from an unmarried mother for seven shillings and sixpence[1] and palmed it upon her husband as her own. Four years later in 1811, the colonel's brother died

[1] In modern terms (1998) seven shillings and sixpence is equivalent to 37·5 pence.

Cuckfield Park

> and the husband and wife with their little daughter, Eliza Ann, took over Cuckfield Park and with it a sizeable fortune. The former coach-builder's wife had her own coach to visit equally wealthy neighbours, and the child grew up and was educated by a private tutor. Until his dying day, only a year later, the colonel believed the little blue-eyed, black-haired girl was his own and he was devoted to her. Eliza Ann grew up and was to have come into the large estate at the age of 21.
>
> But in the background was the colonel's envious sister, who for some reason or other had suspicions that something was wrong. Her husband, the Rev. William Pritchard, sent agents to Dublin and they ferreted out the amazing story. Little Eliza Ann was not an heiress at all. Her real mother was now a Dublin apple-seller who had almost forgotten how she had sold her baby for only three half-crowns. Since the building of Cuckfield Park over 400 years ago there can have been nothing as pitiful there as the plight of Eliza Ann. Brought up to live elegantly and with wealth, she was suddenly plunged into poverty, rejection, and obscurity.

The heart of old England still seems to beat in Cuckfield. This pretty village set like a gem in the lovely Sussex countryside is so unchanged and so unspoilt, that little imagination is required to picture the place as it must have been, one hundred, two hundred, and even three hundred years ago. A former market town, it is our journey's end and it is old, not as old as Clayton and Pyecombe perhaps, but still exceedingly old.

The earliest known spelling of the place was 'Kukefield' in 1091 where it appears in the still existent archives of the Lewes Priory of St. Pancras. Later it was known as 'Cucufelda', and later still, by the charming name of 'Cucufeld'.

The first record relating to the district appears in a charter given by the Earl of Warenne (one of William The Conqueror's generals) to the monks of Lewes Priory. This referred to a gift of land upon which they were to erect a chapel, a building that was to be later replaced by a stone church which now forms part of the present parish church of Holy Trinity.

> Cuckfield is supposed to be the healthiest town in England. The church is one of the most beautiful in England - cared for like a jewel, and the wondrous old houses abutting it would be highly remarkable elsewhere.

These words were by Henry Kingsley, the novelist and brother of the better known author, Charles Kingsley, who moved to the village in 1875 and took up residence at a dwelling called 'Attree'. But quite evidently the health-inducing properties of the district were of little benefit to him, for he died in less than a year, and now lies buried within the shadow of the church that he so admired.

To the north of the village stood the workhouse[1]- an awesome building.

> The big house on the hill – one of the remaining monuments to Cuckfield's greatness.

trumpeted the *Mid Sussex Times* back in 1872. A view unlikely to have been shared by the casual inmates ten years earlier. Then, under the powers invested in them by the New Vagrancy Act, the local authorities could insist that tramps seeking overnight accommodation, be detained for an extra night, and in-between time, made to work in lieu of payment for hospitality received. Not surprisingly the legislation was resented by the travelling fraternity, most of whom regarded the prospect of physical labour as an absolute anathema. The more vocal amongst their number declared that it was little more than slavery, and tore up their clothes as a mark of protest. This resulted in the culprits being dragged before the court, where, according to the following extracts from the records of the old Cuckfield Petty Sessions, they were dealt with most severely:

> (1) Jan. 9th 1883 – John Clarke and John Griffiths, tramps, were charged with tearing up their clothes in the workhouse that morning, and were sentenced to 14 days hard labour.
>
> (2) Jan. 16th 1883 – Wm. Smith (37), James Comber (30), Charles Joice (46), Wm. Clarke (40) and John Harrison (18), tramps, were charged with tearing up their clothes in the union-house that Tues. morning, and the first four were sentenced to 14 days hard labour in Lewes Gaol, and Harrison to 7 days hard labour – Mr King, Labour-master proved the case.

One tramp, having pleaded guilty as charged, was sentenced to six weeks hard labour, upon which he cheekily commented,

> Better say three months Sir, while you are about it.

To which – after conferring with his fellow magistrates – the presiding chairman replied,

> Well, the Bench think you should have what you want, and you will go for three months.

[1] The building still stands. Later it was made into a hospital, and later still was converted into a block of flats.

The White Harte Inn

South Street, Cuckfield

The entrance to the Workhouse

There were of course other establishments in the locality that were happy to provide a traveller with rest and refreshment without the threat of imprisonment, and R. Thurston Hopkins refers to just such one in his book, *The Lure of Sussex.* Apparently he and a friend, whilst on a walking holiday during the early 1920s, were overtaken by bad weather and so sought shelter at the Kings Head Hotel, where to their delight they discovered that a friend of earlier years, one Dick Snow, who formerly held the licence at The Star Inn, Battle, was the landlord in residence:

> "You cannot be dull with Landlord Snow", said Hopkins, "for he is a robust fellow who has the perfect manner of hospitality. In an hour we had received the freedom of the house. Mr Snow dragged us into the Georgian dining-hall to see the old Parliament Clock, and showed us his treasured shovelboard, cut from a tree in Battle Abbey, which must have witnessed the officers of William as they rode hither and thither collecting material for the *Domesday Book.*
>
> "Do you like cider?" asked our host. "I must take you across the way to call on Mr Burtenshaw. Old friend of mine. We'll just trundle over. Come along."
>
> We followed at Snow's heels across the road and up the path of Ockenden Cottage, where Mr Burtenshaw drew us into a cottage with heavily timbered rooms. Ockenden Cottage was once the White Horse Inn, long, long before the King's Head ever existed. The old bottle-glass windows in the interior doors, which date from the 17th century, and the deep hewn cellars suggest its former career. And somehow in a curious, unobtrusive way you feel that Mr Burtenshaw, its present tenant, must be one of the last of a long line of old-time landlords. A fine, grand old gentleman. A good figure of a man!
>
> He talked of the past as men will talk, and one felt that he is the last link with all the real history of Cuckfield. With a deft-handed, kindly gesture, he poured age out of a bottle for us – cider in which lurked all the glory of twenty years' sunshine. Potent stuff it proved to be too, "full of swords and songs" as Mr Burtenshaw remarked. After that glass of cider I saw things, from a mist of vital stillness...

Just a few steps from the King's Head is Ockenden Manor (formerly known as Ockenden House) an ancient building of lichened and weather-worn stone with mullioned windows. Once a school and now a hotel, it was for a century or so before that, the residence of the Burrell family, one of whom, Timothy Burrell, the diarist and lawyer, left a fascinating account of village life between 1688 and 1744. His diary, delightfully decorated with thumbnail sketches and containing ironic and amusing comments, reveals many glimpses of the man's kindly and liberal nature. For instance, he writes:

> Paid John Coachman for a whip to spoil my horses, 1s 6d,"

or

> I payd John Coachman in part of his wages, to be fooled away in cyder or lottery, 5s.

It says much for Burrell's generous spirit, but perhaps less for his judgement, when we learn that despite being aware of his employee's weakness for tipple, he not only continued to engage the man, but actually went out of his way to provide him with funds to obtain liquor. As the following extracts reveal:

> (1) 1705. Pay'd Gosmark for making cyder 1 day, whilst John Coachman was to be drunk with the carrier's money, by agreement; and I payd 2d to the glayser for mending John's casement broken at night by him when he was drunk.
>
> (2) 1706. 25th March. Pd. John Coachman by Ned Virgo, that he may be drunk all the Easter week, in part of his wages due, £1.

John Coachman it must be said came to an entirely predictable end. Whilst driving to Glynde one day (doubtless under the influence of drink) he toppled off the box and onto the road, where he sustained injuries from which he subsequently died. Fortunately his master was unhurt, which was as well, for to the many poor people of the district, Timothy Burrell was a loyal friend. Records reveal that apart from other good deeds, every Sunday morning it was his practice to hand out beef, beer and wheat to all of the needy folk who applied to him. Little wonder then, that after his death, it was officially recorded that he was:

> A great and good man gone, and one by who his counsel and advice, was of great use to us all.

Cuckfield High Street with the Queen's Hall on the left of the picture

The Suffragist March passing through Cuckfield on July 22nd, 1913

Men of the Post Office Rifles who were stationed at Cuckfield during the First World War, parading outside the Rose and Crown Public House. A message on the back of the photograph, quite obviously written by the daughter of the Commanding officer is well worth recording: Isn't this good of Dad? Only half of his company are there, a 140. It's very jolly here. Bank Holiday we motored over to see Auntie Blanche and Mrs B. at Brighton, in the regimental car. We went to a concert in the evening. Yesterday we went to an ' at home' at the Mess which was great sport. I've been very busy taking photos of the men drilling and playing leap-frog"

Our ramble ends with an episode from the great days of Cuckfield's past, the era of the stage-coach, a time when its streets resounded to the clatter of hooves, the rumble of wheels, the peal of post-horns and the ostlers' whistles and cries; a time when over fifty commercial vehicles passed through the town every day, and in so doing, made a great contribution to the welfare of the citizens, and the economy of the community at large.

It was the early years of the 19th century that brought individual fame to the coaches that used the Brighton Road. In particular there was 'The Age', 'The Comet', 'The Quicksilver' and 'The Red Rover'. Of these 'The Quicksilver' was considered the fastest as on average, it covered the distance between London and Brighton in four and three-quarter hours. One of the best known coachmen of the time was Sir St. Vincent Cotton – Vinny to his friends, and 'The Baronet' to the coaching world. He was a fine cricketer and an amateur whip and drove 'The Age' for many years.

Unfortunately, a fondness for gambling led him to ruin, and from thereon, he drove 'The Age', not for sport but a living. To his credit he made no effort to conceal his reduced status, but freely admitted that the job was a necessity, for his income had plunged from £5,000 to a mere £300 per annum. Before he graced the 'bench' (as coachmen called their box seats) 'The Age' was driven by Harry Stevenson, another amateur of renown, and under his influence it became the criterion of the coaching world. The harness was silver plated and the horse-cloths, edged with silver lace, were embroidered with crowns and laurel sprigs. Nor was the passengers comfort neglected, for while the horses were being changed, they were attended by a liveried Guard who dispensed sandwiches and sherry from a silver box. Tragically, Stevenson's career was cut short by fever and it is said that in his delirium, he sat up in bed, and thinking himself on the bench again, cried out.

> "Let 'em go George, I've got 'em!" — then fell back dead.

As was mentioned earlier, the coming of the London to Brighton railway in 1841 sounded the death-knell for the coach, yet for many years it remained a favourite means of transport. Even as late as 1888, one called 'The Old Times' was still running through Cuckfield, and in that year the patrons bet the owners that it could not cover the double journey between Piccadilly and 'The Ship' at Brighton - a distance of one hundred and eight miles- in eight hours. The wager was £1,000 to £500. The bet was accepted, and at 10 am on the 13th of July, 1888, James Selby the coach driver, together with the owners and a few friends were poised to start. The following account of this race against time appeared in the *Sussex County Magazine*.

> The departure from The White Horse Cellars, Piccadilly was at 10 am, Streatham was reached at 10.28, and the horses changed in the amazing time of 47 seconds! Off again at 10.29, they galloped past West Croydon Church at 10.45. Purley Bottom was gained at 10.57, and the flagging horses changed for a fresh quartette in 65 seconds. Merstham, where they halted for two minutes, was left behind at 11.29, and at Horley, where more spirited horses were ready, the timing showed they had covered 28 miles in one hour and fifty-one minutes! The Old Times raced through Crawley at eleven minutes past noon, and then came what might have proved to be a serious setback. The level-crossing gates beyond Crawley were closed. Fortunately, not above a couple of minutes were wasted before they were opened again, and with a rumble, the coach gathered speed to arrive at Peas Pottage where the horses were substituted for others in exactly one minute and five seconds.
>
> Peas Pottage vanished in a cloud of dust at 12.25. Handcross was left behind at 12.33 and Selby reigned in at Cuckfield exactly twenty minutes later. Sixty-eight seconds passed, and with their hooves striking sparks on the cobbles, the horses were away again. Friars Oak was reached at 1.17. Patcham, with more fresh horses in harness was left behind at 1.41, and at 1.56 The Ship at Brighton was in sight. While one of the passengers dashed in for the telegrams that had preceded them, the coach

The King's Head Hotel, Cuckfield, 1904. The coach and horses were owned and often driven by a wealthy American eccentric by the name of Mr Vanderbilt. He was to go down in the British Cunard Liner, the Lusitania *(the largest passenger ship in the world at the time) when it was torpedoed by a German submarine, 1915*

was reversed and the great run to Piccadilly began. There were two stops before they reached Cuckfield at 2.54. Here they paused for but a minute. At Handcross 'The Old Times' passed McCalmont's coach. Peas Pottage was vanishing in the rear at 3.30. Crawley folk heard the pounding of the hooves at about 3.37. Redhill echoed with the galloping of horses at 4.12, and whilst Selby drew up at Merstham for one minute, somebody handed one of the passengers a bouquet. Fifty seconds were all that were required to change horses at Purley. Croydon was skilfully passed in spite of the increase in traffic, and at 5.10, the last change was made at Streatham.

When The Old Times reached the West End, the reception of Victorian London was tumultuous. Police held up the traffic so that the coach might have free passage to hold the precious minutes that had been gained. The upper decks of horse-buses were crowded with spectators waving top-hats and parasols. "Bravo! You'll do it!" yelled the drivers. At exactly 5.30, the sweating horses with Selby still at the 'ribbons', came to a standstill outside The White Horse Cellars. They had covered those one hundred and eight miles in seven hours and fifty minutes. The record had been broken by twenty minutes, and the owners had won the bet of £1,000 with ten minutes to their credit. The cheque that they had won was presented to James Selby as a token of their appreciation and esteem.

We'll not see their like again, those Corinthians of yester-year. Their sparkle and panache exists only between the pages of history books now. But we can at least accompany them in imagination, for they were our forebears. They travelled the road that we have travelled, and their flamboyant spirit surely lingers at every stop and turn of the way, stirring us with memories of a vanished age.

With that our journey is completed, not because there is nothing more to say (for in truth there is plenty yet) but because we should not go on for too long. It was once said that the art of composition is to leave off at such a point that the reader would wish there was more. And in writing this book, we would like to do the same.